The Total Man:

A Complete Guide to Marital Bliss

The Total Man:

A Complete Guide to Marital Bliss

by

D. J. Brown

PICASSO

ENTERTAINMENT

CORPORATION

Visit our Website at

www.picassopublications.com

A Picasso Publications Inc. Paperback

THE TOTAL MAN

This edition published 2002
by Picasso Publications Inc.
10548 - 115 Street
Edmonton, AB, Canada T5H 3K6
All rights reserved
Copyright © 2002 by D. J. Brown

ISBN 1-55279-040-1

Printed in Canada

This book is based on, and structured after,
Marabel Morgan's 1973 bestseller,
The Total Woman.

To the best of my knowledge there is no class or program
entitled **Total Man**, though there probably should be.

The characters portrayed in this book are all fictitious.

No men were harmed in the writing of this book.

CONTENTS

Introduction 1

Part One: Getting Started

Chapter 1   Why Should I Change? 5
                Sarah the Savior. 6

Chapter 2   Liberating The Time. 8
                Your $50,000 Plan 9
                Cutoffs And Sweatshirts. 10
                1-2-3 Business 12

Chapter 3   Interior Re-Decorating 14
                Winning Plans 15
                To Dream the Possible Dream 16
                Pudgies and All 18
                Lesson Number 1 19

Part Two: Getting Down To Business

Chapter 4   Time to Grow Up. 23
                Who's Doing The Housework?. 26

Part Three: Woman Alive

Chapter 5   Accept Her As She Is. 31
                My Wife/My Best Friend 32
                Chocolate, Cuddles and Candlelight. 34
                The Woman Behind The Plan. 36

Chapter 6   Admire Her/Love Her 38
                Heroine Worship 39
                Slender Arms, Overflowing Heart 41
                Rebuilding a Partial Woman. 42

Chapter 7   My Way Or No Way 44
             Oh Queen, Reign Forever. 45
             Wedding Bell Blues 46
             Rockers Away 47
             Yes, I Want To Go Too! 48
             Keep the Fire Burning 50

Chapter 8   Appreciate Her. 51
             Uncaring or Overreacting. 51
             Level of Recognition 53
             Lesson Number 2. 54

Part Four: Sex 101

Chapter 9   Waxing The Car. 59
             Boring To Wow 59
             Welcome Home 60
             Variety Adds Spice. 60

Chapter 10   Bumps In The Bedsprings 63
             Where is the Thrill? 64
             In the Garden. 65
             Yes, Her Too!. 65
             Passing on the Fallacy 66
             Resent Not 67
             Can You Forgive and Forget?. 68
             Fireworks in the Morning/Fireworks at Night. 69

Chapter 11   Sensational Sex 71
             Noontime Delight. 72
             Communication, Not Competition 73
             Lesson Number 3: Sex 101 74

Part Five: Repairing Bridges

Chapter 12   Silence Is Not Golden 77
             Wiser Husbands/Happier Wives 77
             Take a Deep Breath 79

Part Six: Count Your Blessings

Chapter 13 Count Them One By One. 83
            Judge Not. 83
            Praise Her 84
            Love Her 84
            Play Together. 85
            Set Limits 85
            Testing the Waters 86
            Accept Her Friends 87
            Talk to Her. 88
            Encourage Her. 88
            Happy Days. 89
            Child Rearing Rules. 91

Part Seven: Locating Your Source of Power

Chapter 14 Organized Religion 95
            Getting Back to Nature. 96

Part Eight: Physical Fitness and Diet

Chapter 15 Exercise Your Way to Happiness 101
            Healthy Eating. 102
            Figuring Out Fat 104

Conclusion   106

DEDICATION

To Amy, Brandy and Pat
Your love and support give me wings

The Total Man

Introduction

In 1973, during the height of the women's movement, Marabel Morgan wrote a book entitled *The Total Woman*. Ms. Morgan's book was purported to be the final authority on marriage by teaching women to be subservient to their men in every way. The key to a good relationship, according to Ms. Morgan, was sex—and it was up to the woman to "provide" her man with a satisfying sex life by being available to him whenever the urge struck. Not only must she be at her man's beck and call twenty-four hours a day (after all, a woman's duty is to "serve her man"), but she should be creative as well. If he needed costumes and games to keep his sexual interest piqued, she had an obligation to provide them. Nothing must be overlooked in order to keep a man satisfied.

The Total Woman portrayed women as mindless robots, intent on keeping men happy no matter what the cost to their own self-esteem. Ms. Morgan never took into account the reason that so many relationships fail is because many men do not want to put any effort into them. They honestly believe that a woman should feel blessed simply by their presence in her life. The purpose of this book is to let these men know that it is up to them to keep their relationships flourishing by making a concentrated effort to show how much they care every day. They can never assume that women know they are loved; they must demonstrate their love and support through their actions and words. My apologies to Ms. Morgan, as I am sure she had good intentions when she wrote her book. I just have not been able to figure out what they were!

This book is not intended to be the final authority on marriage. I don't pretend to have the answers to all of your marital problems. I do believe it is possible, with a little effort, for any man to have his wife unconditionally respect him in just a few short weeks. He can resuscitate romance; establish open, honest lines of communication; and put a little pizzazz back into his marriage. It really is up to him. He alone holds the key that will unlock the door to marital bliss.

If, through reading and applying these ideas, you become a Total Man, with your wife more confident and satisfied than you ever thought possible, my efforts in writing this book will have been well rewarded (*Morgan 21*).

Part One
GETTING STARTED

1

Why Should I Change?

My spouse and I had been married for ten years and had two small daughters when I lost my job as an executive for a large corporation. Sarah was wonderful: she immediately stepped in and took charge. She began seeing more and more patients in her already busy office (Sarah is a pediatrician). Within a year her practice had doubled and she was forced to add to her large staff. This would mean more money, but it also meant longer hours away from home.

My wife and I had changed roles. She was now earning twice as much money as I ever had, and she was still working outside of the home and I wasn't. I was at home taking care of the kids and the house and making a mess of things. I was resentful of the fact that she had made the transition to sole breadwinner so easily, and I could not adjust to the changes in my life as easily. I subconsciously resolved to make my wife as miserable as I was. In the process, I almost lost her.

I finally realized what a jerk I had become when my parents phoned to tell me they were coming for a long weekend visit. I was determined to have the house spotless before they arrived, and I spent hours cleaning and scrubbing everything in sight. Sarah came home from work that evening and innocently placed her briefcase on the coffee table I had just waxed to a high gloss. I blew up. I ranted and raved and told her how much she belittled my work and didn't have respect for the effort I was making. She listened to my tirade with her mouth hanging open in shock, then said, "You seem to be overreacting to everything these days." She didn't wait for me to respond, but turned and went upstairs to find the kids.

I stood there in shock. Did I really overreact? Didn't I have the right to become angry and let off steam when she did things that displeased me? I sat down at the table and thought about it for a long time. How many times had I come home and tracked mud on a clean floor or left papers strewn about the living room because I knew my wife would pick up after me?

I realized how much I had been harping at Sarah about trivial things, and at that moment I knew that if I didn't change my attitude, I would end up driving a wedge between myself and the woman I loved more than anything in the world. It was not her fault that I had lost my job. She was doing everything she could to keep our family functioning and I was fighting her at every turn.

At that moment I made a vow to become the best man I could be. I did not want my wife to hate me. I wanted to have the best marriage possible and I concluded that it was up to me to make it that way.

Sarah the Savior

My change began with a trip to the library. I read all the marriage manuals and self-help books I could get my hands on. A noticeable pattern began to emerge. Most of these books were directed toward women. They told her how to change to please her man, but very few of them recognized the fact that men need to change too. A good marriage cannot depend solely on the wife giving in to her husband's whims. I decided to apply the principles spelled out in the books to my marriage and the results were astounding.

As I slowly learned to change my attitudes about marriage and women, Sarah began to change as well. She started to talk to me again and confided in me as she did when we had first married. Marriage was fun and interesting again.

After we put the girls to bed at night, we would sit in the living room for hours and talk. She would tell me about her dreams and the goals she was striving toward. I told her what I wanted out of life and she was totally understanding.

We began to smile at each other more often and it hurt me to realize how rare that had become in our house. We had drifted so far apart that the simple act of smiling had almost disappeared. Sarah began to pat my shoulder as we passed each other in the hallway, or she would stop and give me a hug. The kids felt the difference in our attitudes toward each other and they became happier and more relaxed, too.

With the lines of communication reopened, romance was not far behind. I realized that my wife had been yearning for a resurgence of passion as much as I had, but because of my attitude she had been hesitant to approach me.

This new-found love between us has given us a new life together. The result of changing my attitude and applying simple principles to my outlook was so satisfying that I had to pass them on to other men in a Total Man course. Many samples used in this book are taken from the class.

For example, one of my friends, who recently found himself in the same situation I was in, came to the class as a last resort. He and his wife were on the verge of divorce and hadn't spoken a kind word to each other in weeks. One day, their seven-year-old daughter sat at the kitchen table listening to them fight and she finally said, "When I grow up, I don't want to get married. I don't want somebody to yell at me all the time like you and Mommy do." Both parents were shocked and realized what a horrible example they were setting for their child.

At the end of the first class, the husband wondered how he could ever complete the lesson, but he was determined to try. He came to the second class grinning from ear to ear. "I cannot believe what a change has taken place already. When I came here last week, my wife and I were barely speaking, but now it seems as if we're on our way to becoming best friends again!"

Many of my friends wonder why I want to share all of this. Why not let other men make the discovery on their own? I say, ridiculous! If another man can learn from my mistakes and profit by the changes I have made, why not pass it on? Every man deserves the chance to become the best he can be—a Total Man.

2

Liberating the Time

The typical American male should begin every day with good intentions. He was laid off from his job at the power plant three months ago, or his corporation suddenly decided to downsize and his important position as executive vice president has suddenly become unnecessary. He hasn't been able to find any work since. His unemployment check helps, but is not enough to support the family, so his wife has returned to work. Not only is she doing much better than he expected, she has become a vital player for her company and a promotion and a large raise are imminent. They have traded places. She now provides the financial support for the family and it is his job to keep the household running smoothly.

As soon as his wife and kids are out the door, he faces the disaster areas. Each one screams "clean me" or "fix me." What to do first? The grocery shopping on a strict budget set by his wife that does not allow for the daily steaks he craves; the endless errands to buy socks for little Susie or have the cleats replaced for the third time on Bobby's baseball shoes; or making an appointment with the vet, and actually following through this time, to have Barfy neutered because he has jumped the fence four times this month alone and managed to impregnate both Mrs. Peterson's prized poodle and the Jefferson's cocker spaniel?

In the midst of all this trauma, the phone rings. This morning it is a good friend who is having trouble with his wife. Listening to thirty minutes of his buddy's sorrows colors his own situation. He abruptly ends the conversation and looks around him in despair. The morning is half-gone and nothing has been accomplished. "What's the use?" he cries to the empty house. "Nobody appreciates all the work I do around here anyway." Depressed, he pours himself another cup of coffee and sits down at the cluttered kitchen table.

He now has several choices for the rest of the day. He may whine, play the long-suffering saint, or escape with his cold beer and a half-eaten bag of pretzels to his favorite sports channel. When the kids come home at three-thirty demanding snacks, he screams at them because he's mad at himself for forgetting to pick something up at the store.

A lawyer's husband stopped by recently to discuss a problem he seems to encounter every afternoon. His wife has dubbed it "the five thirty syndrome."

"Each afternoon at exactly five thirty," he said, "I drag myself into the kitchen and think, 'Will somebody please tell me what I'm supposed to fix for dinner tonight? And where is that damned cookbook?'"

The syndrome symptoms are rather predictable for the average husband. First, he peeks into the freezer, wishing that there was something in there that his wife had prepared earlier and left for him to heat up. Next, he shuffles through the hamburger helper and the cans of soup in the cupboard, knowing that either of these would elicit an "Again?" from his wife. Frustrated, he gathers the kids into the car, fights the six o'clock traffic to the store, and returns home with a headache and a frozen lasagna that both of the kids said they hated. By the time his wife enters the scene, he is totally fed up. He's too tired to be available to her. He blames her for his mundane existence and takes his frustrations out in other, more subtle, ways. At eleven o'clock he calls one of his friends and discusses an upcoming football game for forty-five minutes while his wife reviews files for an important meeting in the morning. Whenever she makes a suggestive move toward him, he pulls away and tells her that he is trying to talk on the phone.

His wife feels lonely and bewildered inside and thinks, "He doesn't love me anymore." Feeling rejected, she acts distant or grouchy, or sometimes just heads to bed as a protection against constant rejection.

Perhaps you're like many men who say, "I'm sorry, I cannot be available every time my wife is feeling romantic. I have two kids, a dog that has the libido of a sixteen-year-old who just discovered the opposite sex, and there is a yellow, waxy build-up on the kitchen floor that is driving me crazy."

I have known bitter and frazzled men who have been transformed into calm and gentle Total Men! By liberating the time, you too can beat "the five thirty syndrome."

Your $50,000 Plan

When James M. Becker was president of Bender Glass[1], he approached Herman Lee, a management consultant, with a unique challenge: "Show me how to be more productive," he said. "If it works, I'll pay anything within reason."

Lee handed Becker a blank piece of paper. "Write down everything that you need to do tomorrow," he said. Becker wrote. "Now number these items in the order of their importance," Lee continued. Becker quickly wrote again. "First thing tomorrow morning," Lee instructed, "start on item number one and stay with it until it is completed. Next take number two and don't go any further until it is done. Then proceed to number three, and so on. If you don't finish everything on the list, don't worry. At least you will have taken care of the most important things before getting distracted.

"The secret to success is to do this daily," continued Lee. "Evaluate the relative importance of the things you have to get done, establish priorities, record your plan of action and stick to it. Do this every working day. After you have convinced yourself of the value of this system, have your employees try it. Test as long as you like. Then send me a check for whatever you think the idea is worth."

In a few short weeks James Becker sent Herman Lee a check for fifty thousand dollars. Becker later said that this lesson was the most profitable one he had ever learned in his business career.

If it works for a glass factory, it can work in your home factory. This plan is yours for the taking. At no charge, with no obligation! You'll have more time, you'll accomplish much more, and you'll be available for your wife.

Cutoffs and Sweatshirts

If your wife came home in the next thirty minutes, what would she see? Look around right now. Are the beds unmade? Are there toys and dirty clothes strewn from one end of the house to the other? Are there still dirty dishes in the sink and trash piled around, instead of in, the trash can? Don't worry. Here's how you can have it looking fit for a queen and keep it that way, with precious time left over for you.

Take ten minutes now and write down everything you hope to accomplish tomorrow. Don't put it off until in the morning. The day will already be too hectic. Don't worry if the list seems endless. You have a lot of catching up to do.

Just list on one sheet of paper all of those myriad chores that you have been putting off and must do tomorrow (note that you may use both the front and back of your single sheet of paper). A friend of mine keeps his notes on separate post-its. Instead of using a master list, he sticks his notes in every room in the house. He admitted that his daily schedule bounces between chaos and coincidence because the little notes are constantly coming unstuck and he picks them up and sticks them in any convenient spot. It can be confusing when there is a note in the bathroom that says 'empty before defrosting' and he can't figure out what to use to dip out the water and how long it takes before a toilet is completely defrosted. Another friend told me, "I keep a list. But I just keep it in my head and save myself the time it takes to write things down." From now on, write it down. Let your master sheet do your remembering. You have far more important things to remember... like if it's your turn to take the kids to baseball practice this afternoon or is it Mike Turner's turn to drive?

Include yourself on this list. Set aside some time for yourself each day. Include that plumbing project, haircut, working in the yard or just taking a nap.

1. Assign a priority to every item on your list. List these as number one, number two and so on. This may be a good time to decide how important that nap really is!

2. When your wife asks you to do something, she wants it done without constantly reminding you. The next time she delegates a job to you, write it down. Give it top priority on your list. Many women are so convinced that this plan works that now, instead of wasting time asking her husband to do it over and over again, she simply writes it down on his master list.

Assign top priority to the unpleasant tasks like cleaning the toilet and scrubbing the mildew off of the shower tiles. I try to face these in the morning, when I am fresh, instead of late in the afternoon, when I just don't care anymore. A Total Man cannot function properly with nagging thoughts hovering over his head all day. Move to the top of tomorrow's list those things you tend to keep putting off. Don't sweep your weakness under the rug. Just do it!

3. Tomorrow, begin with number one and stick with it until it is accomplished. Remind yourself that if you don't finish it today, you'll just have to do it tomorrow. Don't procrastinate! Then start on number two and stay with that until it is finished. No one else likes to clean out the litter box either, so get it done today! Go to number three and finish it. And so on down the list. Complete each job.

What satisfaction there is in doing a job right the first time and not having to return to it (at least not until next week when you have to do everything all over again)! Early in the day, if you stick to your list and don't get sidetracked by the television, you'll begin to feel a real sense of accomplishment in all that you have done. I love to scratch off each item as I finish it. I feel encouraged to march right down that list (keep telling yourself this and sooner or later you will begin to believe it).

Don't worry if you cannot complete everything on your list. The most important items will have been done. There's no way you could be expected to have accomplished more, and just look at what you did!

4. Keep your daily schedule in a loose-leaf notebook, or draw up a daily calendar on your personal computer and print out your planned activities the night before so you don't forget. This way you keep an accurate record of when you mailed that package, when Debbie's suit went to the cleaners, or when you called the repairman to come out and look at the dishwasher that's had a strange rattle for the last two weeks.

Driving to the store one night last week, Mark noticed a bunch of cars in the parking lot at his children's school. He wondered what was happening, when suddenly, halfway between the school and the grocery store, he remembered. Tonight was his parent teacher conference and he was supposed to meet with Bobby's teacher to discuss reasons why his son may have turned into the class bully! Because he was twenty minutes late already, he raced back to the school and met with the frazzled teacher in his cutoffs and sweatshirt.

The next day he told his Total Man group about the disaster. Instead of using his master sheet, he had stuck a note to the refrigerator and one of the kids used it as a bookmarker!

1-2-3 Business

At the top of my daily $50,000 plan I put, "Prepare dinner after breakfast whether the dishes have been washed or not." When I first came up with this idea I must admit that the thought of it made my stomach queasy. I had always tried to get out of the kitchen as quickly as possible. But I found I could accomplish this goal and have a leg up on dinner as well. Always keep in mind that the more chores you get done early in the day, the more time you will have to spend with your wife and children this afternoon.

You might be asking yourself how I could possibly prepare dinner so early in the day. It's simple, really. First, I asked my wife what she wanted for dinner the night before and wrote it at the top of the list. Each morning I go to the deli and buy the salad, then make a quick stop at the bakery for dessert. Many a Total Man sets the table for his already completed dinner at nine a.m. and never worries about the five thirty syndrome unless, of course, the kids decide to play frisbee with the good china when they come home from school. You can too, if you set your mind to it. You can have all your home duties finished before noon (as long as you're willing to get up at five o'clock every morning). You can have a place for everything and everything in its place.

I am an incurable optimist, but being married to a doctor, I have learned to anticipate every possible problem that might arise in a given situation. I sometimes think, "Whatever can go wrong, will!" With this attitude, it usually does, but it keeps me on my toes. If things go well, I'm surprised. No, I am in total shock. If they don't, I'll put Plan 2 into effect.

Almost every day, things happen that are not on my list. Children get sick, the dog escapes again, the washing machine breaks down and I have twenty girls coming over this afternoon for a scout meeting and I still have to bake cookies. Who knows! Sometimes my wife calls and invites me to lunch. Knowing that life is full of surprises, I try not to panic when someone or something causes me to deviate from my schedule. I try to stay calm by putting into practice Plan 2 (or 3 or 4 or 5 or… depending on how many unseen events crop up during the day). I am learning to welcome interruptions as they help me to realize what a really creative person I am.

A neighbor trudged into my house the other day looking like a really tired John Belushi. He was laughing, not crying, when he said, "Well I'm down to plan 17 now, but would you believe I haven't lost my cool yet? It's amazing how differently I see problems now. It's almost a challenge to see if I can make plan 4 work as well as the original plan. This 1-2-3 thing is like a game I play with the fates of the day and I'm winning." Here was a happy and flexible Total Man. Of course the Prozac his doctor put him on last month didn't hurt!

Those who try this $50,000 plan swear by it. It has changed many lives. If you put it to work for yourself, you'll become more efficient. You will accomplish more than you ever thought possible. With your dinner prepared, you can grab a quick shower while the kids watch cartoons and promise not to hurt each other too badly. You will have energy to spare and pride in yourself that is necessary for happy living.

As for your wife, she will be thrilled. Every woman appreciates order and she will be extremely glad to find it in her own home. She will praise you for your accomplishments, and be pleased with your newfound sense of well being. When you are organized and efficient, her flame of love will begin to burn a little brighter.

Tomorrow is a new day. Wake up to your $50,000 plan!

3

Interior Re-Decorating

Pam and Tony Morrison were returning from the lake with their two little boys. For two weeks, Tony's three-year-old had the allergies and whined and cried constantly. Tony had reacted accordingly. He was extremely frustrated by his lack of rest and relaxation. The entire vacation had been nothing but a bad joke. He hadn't gotten any rest at all. He still got up at the crack of dawn with the kids, did endless loads of laundry and cooked three meals a day (well, okay, two—because he didn't have to cook the cold cereal he served the kids each morning).

To ease the tension among all of them, Pam stopped for lunch at the first McDonald's she spotted from the interstate. Before lunch the family took a walk through a nearby park and cemetery hoping that the kids would be too worn out to fight in the backseat once they returned to the car. Walking through the rows of headstones, Tony read the epitaphs and came upon the grave of a father. The inscription read: He Was The Sunshine Of Our Lives. (*Morgan 35*)

During lunch Tony kept thinking to himself, "If I had a heart attack right here, that would be the last thing Pam would put on my tombstone." From that moment on, Tony decided to do everything he could to become the sunshine to his family and he vowed to forget about the disastrous vacation as soon as possible.

You alone have the power to lift your family spirit or bring it down to rock bottom. You set the atmosphere in your home. If you're happy tonight, chances are your wife and children will be happy too. If you're a grouch, they probably will be too since they take their clues for daily living from you.

How is your attitude toward your daily chores? Are you pleasant to live with, even when your wife doesn't seem to appreciate your efforts? Do you know that your personal happiness depends on you and that no one else is responsible for making you happy? You can decide now on what level you are going to live, despite your wife's attitude. You alone have the power to give yourself total happiness.

One wife said, "I'm tired of paying all the bills. Stop spending so much money!" Her husband's favorite sporting goods store was having a clearance sale so he thought she was deliberately being cheap. He allowed his attitude to register a negative response. He clammed up for days. He had no desire to do anything around the house. The laundry piled up and he didn't care. The kids both had the flu and he didn't want to take them glasses of orange juice. He was worn out both emotionally and physically because his bad attitude controlled his behavior.

This husband's unhappiness could have gone on forever, and would have eventually affected the well being of the rest of his family, but he finally realized that his wife was not responsible for his sense of well being; he was. So what if she didn't want him to shop every day? He had to be honest. If he were in her place he would not want to be paying all of those bills week after week either. He really did have enough golf shirts and two bowling balls are enough for any man. What else did he need? He changed his attitude and changed his life.

A great marriage is not so much finding the right person as being the right person. Most of the men I know would like to improve their roles as husband and father, which are firmly centered around what they do. Their roles as men are something they are and that brings us to the basics.

One man in our class winced and said, "I've got a lot of interior redecorating to do. I guess I'll be busy for awhile." He was right. Interior redecorating of a bad attitude takes awhile, but the results are well worth the effort.

Winning Plans

You can become the sunshine in your home, but you must first learn where the clouds are. Socrates said, "To know yourself is the beginning of wisdom." It's easy to say, but how does one go about understanding himself?

As a starting point, I find that it helps to write down your philosophy of life as a man. This may take some time and effort on your part, but it is beneficial to have in writing your feelings about life. If it's written down, you can refer to your notes whenever you start to doubt who you really are. Don't be shy. Your philosophy may not agree with anyone else's, but that's okay. This is for your eyes only. You do not have to share your notes with anyone else, so be honest. If you cannot be honest with yourself, there is little chance that you will be honest with others.

As a guideline, ask yourself, "Who am I and where am I going? Why am I here? What do I really want out of life?" Taking the time to consider these questions often brings about the answers. Maybe you are really happy being a stay-at-home husband and father. Have you discussed this with your wife? Is she comfortable with being the breadwinner and having you take care of the kids? If this is something that you both agree on, then do it and do it well. Don't worry about what your friends think or what your family will say. If you and your wife are pleased with the decision, that's all that matters.

Perhaps you would like to go back to school. Then do it. Don't make any more excuses. If education is important to you, pursue it. If, prior to losing your job, you had worked as a stockbroker, but you always wanted to be an elementary school teacher, why not be one? If you do not pursue your dreams, the chances of you becoming an angry, bitter man will increase. No marriage can survive such harsh conditions.

One man panicked because he had no philosophy of life. Later he commented that the class assignment was "the greatest challenge of his life. Writing out his ideas forced him to evaluate exactly where he was headed. Now he knows." (*Morgan 38-39*)

If you know anything about the weekly series ER (the show that mesmerizes your wife week in and week out), you know that the doctors always have a plan. This is the only way that they could possibly resolve every crisis that comes their way. Do you have a plan? There is something about a man who knows what he wants out of life that makes him a very interesting partner. How can you become that type of man?

To Dream The Possible Dream

Take a look at yourself. Begin by making a list with four columns: strengths, weaknesses, short term and long term goals.

1. List your strong points. There is potential within you that you have not yet begun to discover. Take a long, hard look at what you do well. What's your favorite hobby? Do your homemaking talents bring you great satisfaction and joy (yeah, right)? Do you have special abilities or education that could contribute to society? If you don't think you do, look deeper. Everybody has something to contribute to society. Use these talents. Develop them. Do volunteer work at the local library or at the elementary school your children attend. Get involved. You can be better than you ever thought possible.

2. What are your weaknesses? List every area in which you do not feel secure. Try to view your weaknesses in light of your childhood. It may have been happy or sad; more than likely it was a combination of the two. Those years had a tremendous impact on the way you react to life today. You brought your childhood reaction patterns with you to your marriage. Keep in mind that you can do nothing to change the past, but you can learn to change the way you react to today's problems. Just because it was a pattern in your family for men to scream and yell when they did not get their own way is no reason for you to behave that way. You have the ability to change. The only thing you need is the desire.

Write down your most embarrassing moments; record your hurts and fears. Recall your moments of success and see how they helped to form some of the strengths you have today. Writing down your past helps you to better understand the man you are today.

Again, there is no reason to show anyone what you have written. This is you at your most vulnerable. Why did you act the way you did? In times of stress did you cry, spend money excessively or lose your temper?

Writing is great therapy and well worth the time and effort it takes. Hidden resentment is like a hangnail. It is a constant hurt that you cannot get rid of. The hurt is always with you. When you finally clip the hangnail, when you face your problems, the sore spot can finally begin to heal.

This exercise may not eliminate your weaknesses, but it may give you the ability to change them into strengths.

3. Write down your short-term personal goals. These are the goals you have set for yourself—not the ones you hope your wife will accomplish. List all of the things you are working toward as an individual. What do you want to accomplish as a husband and father? What do you hope to accomplish as a man?

Try it. Stop reading right now and write down your current goals. Then break them into columns for this week, this month, and this year. Be realistic. One husband told me that he wanted to run a better home, cook more nutritious meals and take better care of himself. The next morning he started his day with a whole new attitude. He felt as if he had goals to work toward.

Another man listed his goals: invite the in-laws to dinner, exercise on a regular basis, stop smoking, and lose weight. When he assigned priorities, losing weight became his main goal. He managed to lose ten pounds in eight weeks. His wife loved his new body so much that she was happy to buy him a whole new wardrobe. You've never seen a more satisfied man.

Your short-term list will also serve as a way to eliminate those things that do not require your immediate attention. Ironing the clothes or walking the dog may be things that you will want to transfer to your $50,000 plan.

4. List your long-term goals. Where do you hope to be ten years from now? Fifteen years from now? Be very specific. List the goals that you hope to reach as a husband and father. You can obtain your goals. Your dreams are not impossible.

Pudgies and All

A young man wrote in his philosophy for class, "I know my wife loves me and I should consider that a blessing. I'm not sure that I love her anymore. I love my children. Maybe it's myself that I don't love. I seem to be living in a dream world and would like to find a way to bring myself into the present."

Many American men of today have never learned to accept themselves. "If only I had the smile of George Clooney or the body of Tom Cruise," they sigh. "If only I had more money, or more time to spend with the kids." If only... What a terrible way to live. Very few men marry millionaires. Very few men look like movie stars. If you cannot learn to love and accept yourself as you are, it is unlikely that anyone else will be able to love you either.

After your shower tonight, look at yourself in the mirror and say, "I accept myself just as I am, pudgy tummy and all." It may not be as simple as it sounds, but it is important. Face each of your physical weaknesses and accept the fact that they exist. After all, you are only human. You, along with the rest of the world, have limitations. Don't be too hard on yourself.

A friend once told me that he felt as if he needed permission "to love myself." It may sound egocentric to love yourself, but it is an absolute must if you ever want to be able to love anyone else, your wife included. Once you learn to accept yourself as you are, you will feel free to be yourself.

Poise and confidence are available to any man. Learn who you really are and where you are headed in life. Develop your own convictions and learn to live by them. More than anything else, learn to enjoy the position you hold in the universe. Remember that there is no one else exactly like you. You are a unique human being.

Understanding and acceptance of one's self may not be easy. It will not happen overnight, but once you begin to accept yourself as you are, you are on your way. You are preparing yourself to reach out to your wife, your children, your friends and the rest of the world.

Lesson Number 1

1. Make a list of everything you need to get done tomorrow. Assign each task a priority and then tackle that $50,000 plan.

2. Write down your life philosophy. Ask yourself three things: Who am I, where am I going, and why?

3. Make a list of both your strengths and weaknesses. Be honest. Then learn to accept your weaknesses and to maximize your strengths. Remember, if your weaknesses can be changed, work at them. Now is your opportunity to improve your life.

4. Set a goal to be reached one week from today. Incorporate this list into your master plan for the week to come.

5. Set one long-term goal and determine how you can make it happen.

Part Two

GETTING DOWN TO BUSINESS

4

Time To Grow Up

You were the quarterback of your high school football team and won an athletic scholarship to a prestigious college, where you promptly pledged the most popular fraternity on campus. You scored three touchdowns in one game, which led your school to the state bowl game, and you helped to win that game, too.

After college, you accepted a cushy job with an advertising firm, where you got through by mentioning your college career to clients who happened to love football almost as much as you did. You dated scads of pretty, empty-headed women and impressed them with your fast car and snazzy clothes.

Then you met the woman you would fall in love with and later marry. She didn't know much about sports and thought athletic scholarships were a real waste of money. You liked her because she was intelligent, and determined to make her own way in the world. She had a job as an assistant editor at a large publishing firm and felt she had a real chance to move up the corporate ladder.

This woman was not impressed by your beer-drinking buddies and thought it was ridiculous that you needed to spend so much time with them—at least one night during the week, and every Saturday and Sunday afternoon to watch the college games and the pro games on your big screen television. She wanted to go to the opera and the ballet and you reluctantly went with her, on occasion.

Your concept of the ideal vacation spot was Cancun, where you could rub suntan oil on your muscles and lounge on the beach and ogle the gorgeous women in their skimpy bikinis. She believed too much sun was bad for your skin and yearned to spend two weeks touring Italy and Greece, but she gave in and went with you to the beach where she spent most of her time huddled under a large umbrella on the patio of the hotel, reading Shakespeare.

Despite your obvious differences, the two of you fell in love and married exactly one year after your first date. She wanted a nice house, with three bedrooms and a pool, in the suburbs where she would feel relatively safe raising the 2.5 children she planned to have. You thought a house was a good investment, so you agreed to buy. You hadn't given much thought to all the work that went along with owning your own home, but you agreed to mow the lawn every Saturday morning (before your buddies came over with their wives to watch the games).

She kept the house spotless and cooked dinner every night of the week. On weekends, she made potato salad, macaroni salad, two pies and homemade ice cream to go with the burgers you threw on the outdoor grill at half-time. After the last game, you magnanimously invited everyone to enjoy a dip in the pool. Since your wife didn't like to swim, she was left alone in the kitchen week after week to clean up the mess and offer cold drinks to anyone who sauntered in, dripping puddles of chlorinated water on her freshly waxed floor as they lingered to tell her, one more time, what a great guy you were and how lucky she was to have found you.

During the week, both of you spent thirty minutes in morning rush hour traffic to get to your jobs in the city. You both left your respective offices at five, but it took her much longer to get home than you because she stopped to pick up the dry cleaning (most of it yours) and groceries.

When the kids, a girl and a boy, came along, it was your wife who arranged for child care, took them to the pediatrician whenever necessary, fed them, bathed them, dressed them and tucked them in to bed every night.

Suddenly she is telling you that she cannot handle everything alone anymore and she wants you to start pitching in, or else. What does she want from you? You go to work every day, you don't drink excessively or waste money on gambling (well, there is the occasional bet on a game or two, but that doesn't count). She was the one who wanted the house and the kids, shouldn't she be the one who takes care of them? After all those things are women's work, right?

Wrong! Your wife wants you to grow up and learn some responsibility. Maybe she was the one who pushed for the house and she wanted children more than you did, but you both agreed to buy a home and have kids so it is up to *both* of you to take care of them. It's nice to spend time with your friends, and your wife does not expect you to give them up entirely, but she does expect you to help with preparation and clean up whenever the two of you entertain.

During one class, I asked my students to describe a typical day in their households. Following is a composite of the information we compiled:

The alarm rings at five thirty and you roll over and cover your head with a pillow as you hear your wife stumble from the bed and head for the bathroom. There is still an hour and a half before you have to get up.

The two of you have been married for a number of years and you know her routine by heart:

1. She takes a quick shower, blow-dries her hair, puts on her make-up, dons the suit, sans jacket, she has chosen for the day, and slips her feet into a pair of scruffy slippers.

2. As she leaves the bathroom she will pick up her wet towel, along with the one you wadded up and tossed in the corner last night. Before she leaves the bedroom she will also stop at the foot of the bed to pick up the clothes you left scattered there because you were just too tired to put them in the hamper before you went to bed.

3. She will go downstairs, start a load of laundry, brew a pot of coffee and go out and retrieve the newspaper from the rosebushes where the paperboy insists on tossing it every morning.

4. She pours a cup of coffee, butters a piece of toast and hurriedly consumes both of them while glancing through the front section of the paper. By this time the laundry is done, so she tosses that in the dryer, then heads back upstairs to wake three-year-old Joey and his six-year-old sister, Kate.

The kids whine and complain because it's early and they're tired, but she manages to get them both dressed and takes them downstairs for breakfast. Inevitably, one of them will spill something on their clean clothes and have to be brought back upstairs to change.

5. She makes another trip downstairs, puts the dog out in the backyard, lets the cat in, washes the breakfast dishes, packs Kate's lunch, finds Joey's tennis shoe that has somehow gotten wedged behind the refrigerator, and takes a package of chicken breasts out of the freezer so they will be thawed in time for dinner.

It is now seven o'clock. You get up, put on your bathrobe and stumble down the stairs. Once in the kitchen, you pour yourself a cup of coffee, pull the sports section from the paper, scattering advertisements across the floor, where you leave them, and plop down in your chair at the table. Your wife has dashed back upstairs to make the beds, retrieve her jacket and put on her shoes. The kids are making too much noise, so you stick a Disney movie in the VCR and tell them to sit down and watch it quietly.

Your wife comes back into the room, grabs her briefcase and Kate's lunch, tells both kids to hurry because they are running late, kisses your cheek, and heads for the front door. Just as she is about to exit, you remind her to pick up your good suit at the cleaners on her way home. She will drop Joey off at his daycare and Kate off at the elementary school where they offer before-school care. She will then spend thirty minutes in traffic, commuting to work.

You, in the meantime, have finished reading the paper, eaten two bowls of cereal, drank two more cups of coffee, leisurely gotten dressed and strolled out the door for a quiet ten-minute drive to the office. Aahh! What a way to start the day!

Your wife leaves work at five o'clock, stops to retrieve the kids at the daycare center, picks up your dry-cleaning, stops at the grocery store for milk, bread and whatever else is needed this evening. She arrives home at six, fixes the kids a snack, spends thirty minutes listening to them tell her about the day, and begins to prepare dinner.

You arrive home at six-thirty, change clothes, flop down on the couch with the remote, holler at the kids because you cannot hear the news, and remain on the couch until your wife tells you that it is time to eat.

After the meal, she does the dishes, gives both children a bath, reads them two bedtime stories, sends them downstairs to kiss you goodnight, and tucks them in with last drinks of water and lots of hugs and kisses. You, in the meantime, have fallen asleep in front of the television and will stay there until she wakes you to let you know it is time to go to bed. Man, what a rough day you've had!

Does any of this sound familiar to you? It does? And you're still married? Maybe your marriage vows were different from mine, because I don't recall anything that told my wife to "Promise to cook, clean, bear and raise children, all without complaint or assistance from this day forth." I am sure if the preacher had uttered those words, my bride would have run screaming from the church!

Who's Doing the Housework?

Now is the time for reassessment. If your life resembles the above scenario in any way, it is time to make some changes. Your wife is going to work every day just like you are. She is also doing the cooking, the cleaning, the shopping, and taking care of the kids. What are you doing? Granted, you mow the lawn once a week and change the oil in both vehicles when they need it, but are you helping with the routine, day to day chores?

The biggest problem women face is finding the time for both house-work and paid work. Most men and women believe that working couples need to share household responsibilities, yet the burden of taking care of the home and family continually falls on the woman. It is also interest-ing to note that "employed wives average two to three times the number of hours of domestic/childrearing work as their husbands." (*Chafetz, 116*) Contrary to what we believe, we are not making women's lives eas-ier; rather we are forcing them to work harder than ever before.

Table 4.1 shows how couples in which both partners hold full-time jobs divide the housework. Two things stand out: "Women and men do different tasks, and women clearly spend more time than men on domes-tic tasks." (*Reskin and Padavic, 149-150*) Men spend more time doing chores that can be postponed if necessary. If a man is busy, the oil in the car can be changed next week or the week after. If he's tired, the grass can always be cut next weekend. Maybe it will be so long that the kids hide in it because they don't want liver for dinner, but that's okay because you know they'll come back in the house when they get hungry.

Table 4.1
Time Spent on Household Tasks by Full-Time Workers
Measured in Hours per Week, 1987

Household Tasks	Men	Women	Men as a Percentage of Women
Preparing Meals	3.0	8.0	37.5
Washing Dishes	2.3	5.2	44.2
House Cleaning	2.1	6.6	31.8
Outdoor Tasks	4.9	2.1	42.8*
Shopping	1.7	2.9	58.6
Washing, ironing	1.0	3.8	26.3
Paying bills	1.6	2.0	80.0
Auto maintenance	2.0	0.4	20.0*
Driving	1.2	1.7	70.6

*Women as a percentage of men.

Source: Beth Anne Shelton, Women, Men, and Time: Gender Differences in Paid Work, Housework, and Leisure. New York: Greenwood Press (an imprint of Greenwood Publishing Group, Inc., Westport, CT), 1992, p. 83. Reprinted with permission of the author.

A woman's chores do not allow her the luxury of postponement. The dishes must be washed on a daily basis or the kitchen will soon be overrun with bugs. The laundry needs to be done every few days or everyone will soon be running around naked. Groceries have to be purchased if the family plans to eat, and the bills must be paid unless you want the electricity turned off and your car repossessed.

The question you need to be asking yourself at this point is, "Am I doing my fair share?" When was the last time you washed dishes or did a load of laundry? Can you make a bed and write a check? Of course you can! You are a grown man. It is time to start participating in the care of yourself and your family. If you got married simply to have someone else do all of the housework, you would have been better off hiring a housekeeper or using a weekly maid service. You married your wife because you loved her and she made you happy. It will take some time to change the attitudes you have lived with for years, but keep reminding yourself that housework is not woman's work. It is the work of everyone who lives in the home. Do your part!

No one expects you to take on all of the household chores, but no one wants you to do just the easy tasks either. Cleaning the toilet and scouring the tub are not pleasant jobs, but learn to do them anyway. Don't take on only the simple chores like running the vacuum. Anyone can do that. Pitch in and help out with the things that take time and effort.

Help take care of the kids, too! Remember, your wife did not have them by herself and it should not be her job to raise them by herself. You can change a diaper and wipe vomit off of the baby's chin. Yes, both of them smell bad and make you feel like you might throw up yourself, but, with a little practice, you can get used to it.

You don't honestly believe that your wife enjoys those tasks, do you? She likes the baby after she has been bathed and powdered the same as you do, but someone has to make the effort to keep her smelling sweet. Why not make that one of your chores? Get involved in your children's lives while they are young. The one who will benefit most will be you!

If you get involved with the housework, as unpleasant as it may be, your wife will have more time and energy for you. Isn't that what you want?

Part Three

WOMAN ALIVE

5

Accept Her As She Is

Bill and Carrie are newlyweds. I've known them both since college and have been witness to their marital highs and lows. Bill took the Total Man class and wrote to me several weeks ago to tell me about his results.

"Three years ago," he wrote, "I watched Carrie walk down the aisle to say 'I do,' but I was already wondering how I could redo. I began subtly at first, then confronted her head-on. That's where our problems began. Since I took your class, I've stopped nagging Carrie and started accepting her for what she is. She's like a new woman and we're like a new couple! Thanks so much for the class!" (*Morgan 51*).

It's true that most of us marry a woman assuming that we can change the things about her that we don't like. Then we spend years of married live attempting to do just that. Why are we such idiots? It never works! The poor woman crawls into a protective shell and vows never to try to communicate with the Neanderthal that she married.

A woman needs to be accepted as she is. Exactly as she is. Don't ever say things like, "Sure your hair looks nice, but isn't it a little short?" Or, "Did that dress shrink? It looks just a little snug around your hips." She wants total acceptance. This will do more than anything else to convince her you really love her. Her desire for total acceptance shouldn't seem strange. I need to feel accepted too. Don't you? Do you want your wife to constantly nag and criticize you? No, you do not! Give her the same respect that you want for yourself.

Do you have a good friend who will listen to you and accept you no matter what? I do. We can sit on the patio with a couple of beers or talk as we repair one another's cars and I feel free to tell him anything. I can be myself without fear of rejection or unsolicited advice. Sometimes he laughs at me, but I do the same to him. I know he doesn't mean anything by his laughter. Men sometimes have a hard time expressing their emotions and laughter can help to ease the tension. That's acceptance. He cares about me no matter what and I care about him too. Although we may often find it difficult to let each other know how we feel, we work at it and accept each other.

Can you do less for your wife? Can't you accept her as you would your best friend? Your wife needs your acceptance in the same way. If you do this, she will not be able to find enough hours in the day to spend with you; she will want to be with you more and more. The barriers you have built up over the years will surely begin to fall away.

My Wife, My Best Friend

Unfortunately, I'm a complainer by nature. I honestly don't mean to be; it just worked out that way. Complaining is my occupational hazard. All day long I bark orders at my kids: "Pick up your clothes. Put that damn dog outside! No, you can't have another cookie, you already ate six. Hang up the phone. I said hang up the phone. No, not five more minutes! Hang it up now!" When my wife walks through the door, I continue the tirade: "Don't leave your briefcase there; I just washed that. Call your mother; she's lonely." And on and on.

For four years I nagged my wife about the same things every day. She finally got to the point where she couldn't take it any longer. "Stop complaining all of the time! I heard you the first time! I am not your child, I am your wife!"

I was thunderstruck by her words at first, but I couldn't seem to get them out of my head. I felt helpless. How would the buttons ever get sewn back on my shirts if I wasn't supposed to remind her about it at least four times a day? How could she be so mean? I was only trying to be helpful!

I thought back over the previous week and replayed some of our more intense arguments (hitting the freeze-frame when I needed a minute to remember what we had been discussing). I noticed that my wife's reactions to my complaining always fell into a predictable pattern. If I complained continuously for two hours, she would begin to ignore me. If she didn't ignore me, as she usually did, she exploded.

"You're always reminding me about those damned buttons," she said. "You've told me about them four times already tonight. I always sew them on, but I refuse to do it again until you quit bothering me! It's not like you need dress shirts right now anyway! You're not going anywhere!" I should have known that would happen. Every time I back her into a corner, she comes out fighting!

According to some psychiatrists, I was beginning to sound like her second father, and there was no way she would ever feel romantic toward her second father. I realized that if I continued to complain, I would alienate her even more. I also realized that if I kept pushing on an issue that wasn't important, it may lead to resentment and/or retreat to the gym, the office, or even another man, one who knew how to sew on his own buttons!

One thing was certain. My complaining wasn't leading to a mutually acceptable solution. I decided that night not to complain to my wife about missing buttons ever again. If she didn't want to sew on buttons, maybe I could learn to do it myself. If I couldn't do that, maybe I could squeeze a few new shirts into my clothing allowance. It turns out that I didn't have to worry. She sewed on those buttons for me the very next night without my saying a single word about it. Amazing! Women can manage to do their chores without constant reminders from us.

Then I decided to try to stop complaining altogether. Instead, I would stuff a snack into my mouth every time I felt the urge to criticize (something low fat of course). I would simply remind her once and then the decision as to whether or not she wanted to do her chores was hers. I finally realized that my woman's home is her castle; at least it should be. She should feel comfortable enough in the privacy of her own castle to do whatever she wants. If she wants to leave her dirty clothes and wet towels in a pile in the bathroom she should be allowed to. If she wants to keep the kids up until midnight watching reruns of "I Love Lucy" and leave it to me to drag them out of bed in the morning to get ready for school, she should. Complaining to her over trivial events will only make her angry.

A frustrated husband once wrote to a well-known advice columnist[2] asking her to praise husbands for complaining to wives if their health was at stake. "The husband," the writer stated, "should complain if his wife has gained ten pounds since they married (even though he may have put on twenty-five), if she drinks too much at parties and he has to drive her home, or if she isn't exercising enough (although the only exercise he gets nowadays is bending over to retrieve dirty socks from under his son's bed)." The man ended his letter on a pleading note, "Please tell men everywhere who love their wives to complain to them. It could add years to their lives."

The columnist's reply was wonderful. "Who wants more years like that? Sorry, I don't agree. Complaining never kept anyone alive. It has, however, killed many marriages."2

If you have a real emotional need to complain, it might be safer to call a buddy and use him as a sounding board. Choose someone who won't tell his wife, who will, in turn, tell yours. Release your frustrations with him instead of with your wife. A whiny, complaining man doesn't make for a long marriage or a happy wife.

Complaining is the total opposite of acceptance. If you are in the habit of complaining, you know how hard it is to quit, but do it anyway! I am not saying that it will be easy. You will have to work at it. One thing that I did was to charge myself a quarter every time I complained unnecessarily about something. Those quarters went into a jar on top of the refrigerator and, at first, they added up quickly. Once I realized just how often I complained, I was embarrassed. Proof of my bad behavior made me more determined to become a new man. You will find that once you learn to accept your wife, faults and all, you will no longer feel the urge to criticize. Just the thought of no more nagging may send her into raptures.

One husband who kicked the habit after ten years reported that "the most wonderful thing has happened. Her faults really don't seem to bother me anymore. I simply concentrate on all of her good qualities and I love her more than I ever did before." He paused for a moment. "She seems to love me more too," He said at last. The joy in his voice was music to my ears.

Chocolate, Cuddles and Candlelight

Your wife is who she is. Accept her. This idea is as old as life itself. God loves us exactly as we are. Even if we don't deserve it, He still cares. His love is total and unconditional. Because God loves us, with his help we can love and accept others, especially our wives.

One man refused to go along with this idea. "I don't love my wife anymore," he complained bitterly. "She doesn't deserve to be accepted." This seems to be the rule rather than the exception in many marriages. What's the answer to the wedded bliss blues?

First of all, the Bible teaches us that husbands and wives should love one another. If you have lost the love for your wife, why not ask God to help you regain it? Secondly, if you want your marriage to last, you must learn to accept her. Your relationship will not flourish if you don't. The choice is yours and yours alone. You can go on living with resentment and anger or accept your wife as she is.

If you choose anger, you may not have a marriage to worry about anymore. If you choose to accept your wife, where do you start? It's simple really. All you have to do is make up your mind and do it. Remember that this is still the woman you married, the woman you promised to love "till death do us part." Maybe she has gained a few pounds or her hair is turning gray—so have you and you still want acceptance. Inside she still possess those qualities that made you fall in love with her in the first place. Don't try to change her. That's the highest form of love there is.

The change I noticed in one couple was amazing. The husband put a lot of thought into this decision. But once he made up his mind the wife noticed the difference immediately. "She has changed so much," he bragged to me. "She has become the loving and caring woman she was when we first got married. She wants to give me all of her paycheck all of the time. I think I may start taking it... Just to make her happy of course!"

All kidding aside for a moment, there is a logical reason that his wife changed. She knew that she was loved exactly as she was. In return she was able to offer her spouse the love and acceptance that he craved too. This is definitely a two way street!

Some men don't complain verbally, but they let their aggravations be known in other ways. He sighs loudly as he stands before the sink with his arms buried to the elbows in bubbles. "I do accept my wife," he tries to convince himself. "I've been putting up with her eccentricities for years. I don't ever complain and I won't start now. I'll just stay with her because of the kids."

Tolerance and acceptance are not the same thing. Your saintly tolerance only tends to make your wife feel guilty and unlovable. She can sense that you are not accepting her and she is unable to love you as much as she would like.

Your wife needs your acceptance especially at times when she feels she hasn't done her best. If she's already feeling blue, don't make it worse. Never, ever compare her to another woman. This definitely includes your mother, your grandmother, and any other female relatives who may have qualities that you admire as well as women whom you've only glimpsed on television. Remember, she will never feel comfortable enough to confide in you if she thinks you're always comparing her to someone else. Life is too short to spend all of your time wishing for things that you can never have. Concentrate on your wife's good qualities and give her ego a boost when it needs it.

Your woman needs to feel loved and needed every day of her life. If you won't accept her eccentricities, who will? A Total Man caters to his wife's little whimsies whether they be in her desire for extra chocolate chip cookies, cuddling before she falls asleep at night, or candlelight with dinner. He makes her home into a safe harbor, a place where she can retreat when the world seems to be pressing in from all sides at once.

The Woman Behind The Plan

Having lived on both sides of the fence, being both the provider and the providee, I know where the greener pastures are. During the early years of marriage I was determined to mold my wife into the woman I thought she should be. One thing that I found particularly irritating was that she spent hours on the computer every night buying stock options. I was jealous of the time she spent on the computer and I was also a nervous wreck thinking she would make a bad choice and lose all of our money.

One day a good friend of my wife's, who happened to be the one who set up her computer and told her where to check out stocks, called me. She knew my wife was at work and she wanted to give me some advice. "Let your wife do whatever she wants on her computer. Don't even try to tell her what she can or cannot do with her money. You stay out of it and take care of the house."

I was furious at both of them! How dare my wife talk about me to someone else and how dare that someone else feel she had the right to call me and tell me what to do? But that woman had sensed my resentment. She knew that I wasn't allowing my wife to feel comfortable in her role as provider.

My attitude has changed, and my wife and I are both happier because of it. I have decided to support my wife's plans and if that becomes too difficult, I will continue to be supportive of the woman. When I lost my job, she was there for me and never put me down or called me a failure. Can I really do less for her?

If you make this decision, be sincere. Your wife will be appreciative of your change in attitude but she may be suspicious at first. She may be wondering what you are up to now. Her love cannot be won by someone who is trying to be manipulative. Be sincere, be persistent, and, above all, be patient. You did not become the man you are overnight and you cannot expect her to believe you really want to change just because you do or say one nice thing.

One husband berated his wife, "I've had a new attitude for the last week and you haven't even noticed." She responded, "You've made changes before. I think I'll wait to see if this one will be permanent before I react." Her love had been challenged so many times over the years than it would take more than a single effort on her husband's part to convince her.

Once you begin to accept your wife, you can stop worrying about being her advisor. After all, she has been making her own decisions for a long time. She doesn't need your advice, she needs your acceptance. The pressure to provide good advice will be lifted instantly from your shoulders, not to mention the pressure lifted from hers! She will probably begin to seek your opinion and allow you access to the computer once in awhile!

Accepting your wife is the first step in making your woman feel totally alive and free to live her life as she sees fit. It allows her to become a Total Woman. She has the potential, but cannot obtain it until you allow her to relax and be herself. Accept her just as she is. Accept both her strengths and weaknesses from this day forward.

6

Admire Her/Love Her

A woman's most basic needs, outside of a satisfying sex life, are acceptance and admiration. Men need to be loved, but women need to be admired. As men, we should remember this one important difference between the genders.

A few days ago a man told me that his wife did not fulfill his needs. "She never tells me she loves me," he sobbed. "She never shares her feelings with me. She's as cold as the Thanksgiving leftovers at the bottom of the deep-freeze."

Your woman, like so many other American women, may have learned to hide her true emotions. She may be tired of trying to share love and being told to "prove it" by providing trinkets and gadgets as symbols of her affection. Remember that she has been brought up in a culture that has taught her expressing her emotions will only get her stepped on and kept down. Grown-ups were too busy pursuing their own dreams to listen so she learned to keep her emotions to herself.

We men, on the other hand, believe it is our God-given right to throw tantrums and let everyone know how we really feel about everything. We grew up full of passion and were taught that it was perfectly okay to express it. We became adults and that's when the real fun started. Ms. Cool wed Mr. Passion. Is it any wonder that he felt unfulfilled because she refused to lay her heart out on the table where he could crush it with one blow from his balled up fist?

Do you find yourself wondering why your wife doesn't melt like butter when you tell her you love her? Try saying "I admire you" instead and see what happens. She may want to know what it is that you're admiring. Be honest. Tell her how much you admire her business sense, how you admire the way she stepped in and took over when you lost your job, and how you revere the way she never seems too tired at night to read that one last story to the kids before they go to sleep. Let her know how much you appreciate everything she does for you and watch her eyes light up. Once she realizes that you are serious she will begin to give you the love and affection you have been yearning for.

As a man you want to be loved by that woman, right? She, being a hard-working woman, needs to be admired and respected by you. Her needs come first. Some men are irritated by this idea until they realize that they've been given almost everything they ever wanted their entire lives. It is time to put someone else's needs first. It is an admirable quality, not a fault, to be able to put another person before yourself.

You are the person your wife needs to make her feel special. She married you because she thought you were a good man. She may receive promotions and raises, but without your genuine admiration she has no motivation. You are the one who has the ability to build her up and keep her going day after day.

A young teacher was starved for admiration from her husband. He wanted her to fulfill his needs without him fulfilling hers first. He expected applause for every plate he washed and every meal he cooked. "Why should I have to tell her how I feel first?" he questioned. His wife threw herself into her work and began bringing more and more papers and essays home to grade every night. The husband's selfishness only served as a barrier between them.

During a Total Man class, this husband realized just how selfish he had been and made a vow to change. He began to tell his wife how much he admired her and their relationship began to change. One afternoon she said, "I don't know what happened to you, but I appreciate how much you do around the house. You seem so much happier for some reason."

Heroine Worship

Try this simple test for one week. It will not hurt you or cost any money. Starting tonight, begin to admire your wife. Determine to meet her needs before your own. Remember that honesty will encourage her to share her thoughts and feelings with you.

Pay attention when she talks to you. Let her know you are really interested. Turn off the television, lay down the sports page and make eye contact. Even if you don't care if Dr. Greene got beat up in the bathroom or Carol and Doug may start their relationship again, listen to what she is saying. Make her interests your interests.

Don't interrupt or become preoccupied. Participate in the conversation. Indifference will make her stop talking to you because she will know you don't care. A friend called me the afternoon his wife filed for divorce. When he asked her why, he was flabbergasted by her response: "You've always been indifferent to me. You never cared about what I wanted or knew what I was interested in."

Good marriages require tact: the ability to view another person as she views herself. Your wife needs you to see her as she sees herself. Take a good look at her. She loves her body; it's the only one she has and it's been through a lot with her. She wants you to love it too. The only way she'll ever know that you do is if you tell her. She may not believe you at first, but tell her anyway! If those little dimples behind her knees have always sent shivers down your spine or you adore her long, slender neck, tell her. Tell her! Then tell her again! Pretty soon she will start to believe you really mean it.

This may seem ridiculous to you. She knows she has pretty hair and a great smile; why does she need to be told? If this is true, your wife is long overdue for some admiration. It should be considered a privilege for you to assure her that she looks as good as she always hoped she could.

When she comes through the front door tonight really look at her body. It may have been years since you really saw your wife. Try looking at her through another man's eyes—her assistant's or the bag boy at the local grocery store. If you don't start admiring her and paying attention to her, someone else might!

Tell her you love her body. You may feel silly at first, but practice until it sounds natural and sincere. If you haven't praised her lately, she is probably starved for admiration. Don't try to tell her everything that you admire about her all at once or she won't believe you. Remember, it's been a long time since you've said anything nice about the way she looks. Give her one, honest compliment a day and watch her begin to bloom right in front of your eyes. Aren't you a lucky man?

Look for her admirable qualities. Even the plainest woman has certain qualities that are worth admiring, but we are talking about the woman you married. Compliment the woman who used to make your heart pound madly in your chest simply by brushing a lock of hair out of her eyes. Admire the woman who made you feel warm all over whenever she laughed at one of your jokes. Who knows—she may decide to make you feel warm all over tonight!

It is not enough, however, to admire her body; you must also admire her mind. This is the woman who stepped in and took over when you believed the family was headed for the poor house. She's the one who assured you that everything would be all right, and she was right. She has become a successful businesswoman and she did not do that by being a fool. She is a bright, highly motivated woman and you know it. When was the last time you complimented her on her abilities and achievements? These qualities are surely worth noting and are much more important to her than her appearance.

Slender Arms, Overflowing Heart

Admire her personally. This is what she longs for. When she comes home tonight would you rather have her compliment your freshly waxed car or tell you how nice you look? She would rather be given a personal compliment than told how great her company is to keep giving her a paycheck week after week.

When your wife gets ready for work tomorrow, watch her as she looks at herself in the mirror. She sees a mature woman with nice hair and clear skin. It doesn't matter if she's gained a few pounds here and there—she still looks good and she wants you to notice. That really isn't so strange. Do you want her to point out that you're now wearing your pants well below your waistline (otherwise you'd be buying a bigger size) or that your forehead seems to have gotten larger in the last few years? You want her to concentrate on your good qualities, and that's exactly what you should do for her.

A husband told me he had once blurted out one night as his wife was getting ready for bed, "Look at you! You're getting fat and you've got varicose veins! We might as well face it, you're not a young girl anymore." The first shot had been fired. His wife was devastated and to protect herself, she brutally ticked his faults off on her perfectly manicured fingers. She could not respond rationally to his insults so she struck out at him in a way that she knew would hurt him as much as he had hurt her.

In class one day I gave the assignment for the men to admire their wives' bodies. One man went right to work on his homework. His wife was taller than he and never wore heels because she didn't want to intimidate him. In all their years together, he had never told her how much he admired her height and how good her clothes, no matter what she wore, looked on her. It was a giant step for him. That night as she was going over briefs for a court case the next morning, he sat down on the couch next to her and handed her a gift-wrapped box. When she opened it, she was surprised to see a pair of high heels inside. "I love that you're so tall," he whispered shyly. She smiled and bent over to plant a kiss on the top of his head. "I love you, too," she said.

By the way, compliments can work wonders for your children too.

The couple in the example above has a thirteen-year-old daughter who is as tall as her mother and often feels awkward because she towers over all the other kids at school. Her father was working in the garage one day and needed a can off of a high shelf. He was about to get the ladder when he spotted his daughter slouching against the side of the house. "Becky," he called. "Can you come here and help me?" The child handed him the can and he expressed his gratitude. "You know," he confided. "I've always wished I was tall like you and your mother. It must be nice to be able to reach things and to have other people need your help." Becky has been standing a little taller ever since.

Your wife won't mind helping you either if you approach her in the right way. Instead of struggling to peel those potatoes, why not ask her to chip in and help because you know how fast she is with the potato peeler? She doesn't mind lending a hand.

I have only ever heard of one case where this principle backfired. One husband asked his wife to help him every time he peeled potatoes and she became suspicious. "What is going on here?" she asked. "You've been peeling potatoes for years and never had any problem before." Don't over do it. Ask for her help only when you really need it.

Rebuilding a Partial Woman

I overheard one husband say that he felt ridiculous practicing things to say to his wife. "It doesn't seem honest," he said. "Anyway, her body's not that great anymore. Why should I have to lie to make her feel better? Isn't there a way that I can be truthful and still fulfill her needs?"

I am not promoting lying in order to give your wife's ego a boost. She is not a fool and would see through false flattery instantly. I am saying that she has a deep-seated need for honest and sincere admiration. Surely there is something about your wife that you admire—be it her flair with clothes, the way she fixes her hair each day, the beautiful smile she frequently flashes your way, or the way she can balance the checkbook to the penny in fifteen minutes flat. There is always something to admire if you will look for it.

If the lines of communication between you and your wife have shut down, you may have trouble at first finding something nice to say. If this is the case, think back to the days when you first realized she was the woman you wanted to spend the rest of your life with. What were the things that you loved about her then?

An older couple had stopped communicating so long ago that he couldn't think of anything to admire about her anymore. He thought back to the days when they were a struggling young couple, he in law school and she working two jobs to support them. He warily mentioned to her how much he had admired her determination and stamina in those long ago days. Those were the first kind words she had heard in years and her reaction astounded him. Her eyes filled with tears and she couldn't find the words to express her appreciation. The husband was touched that such a little remark about a time so long ago touched her so deeply. It was a real turning point in their marriage.

A marriage must not be allowed to stagnate. In order to have a long and successful marriage, you must keep it growing. Think of it as tending a garden. You treat the tender, new buds with gentle care, but you pull the weeds, not wanting them to have a chance to take root and spoil the beauty of the flowerbed. At the end of a long, hard day is when your wife really needs your compliments and admiration. Put her shattered ego back together again at the end of the day. That's not lying, that is the very essence of the love you should be sharing.

Life is made up of seemingly unconnected events, but often it is something little that can change things forever. Behind every successful woman is a man, encouraging her and meeting her needs. There may be some exceptions to this, but I would be willing to bet they are few and far between. Remember, what complaining and whining cannot accomplish, love, admiration and acceptance can!

7

My Way Or No Way

What seems to be the greatest cause of problems in a marriage? I find that the villain, in most cases, turns out to be a clash of egos. Your opinion versus her opinion. If they happen to be the same—fine, wonderful. You can skip this section and move on to the next. If not, what started out as a simple conflict may erupt into a full-blown battle of wills.

Your wife comes home from the office longing for a cold glass of wine and a hot bubble bath. You, on the other hand, have been cooped up all day with two small children with the chicken pox and the attention spans of... well, of little kids! Instant chaos ensues. Both of you start shouting and nothing gets accomplished. Maybe there's a little extra money and you want to take a well-deserved vacation, but she wants to replace the worn out tires on her car. Another conflict.

All couples have these problems. How can these conflicts be resolved? Some couples never learn to compromise and the only alternative left to them is to go their separate ways, instead of learning to give in once in awhile.

If you have no desire to compromise every now and then, the best alternative for you is probably to remain single. If you are married, and not learning to compromise, you have probably already reached the conclusion that marriage is not an easy feat.

You may think the solution is simple. Your wife should give in to you, right? You are the man and she should respect your opinions. Wrong! Unless both of you are willing to give in to the other's desires once in a while, your marriage is doomed. Men are not the lords and masters of their homes. Wives are equal partners and their opinions should count just as much as yours. I cannot stress strongly enough that the key to a successful marriage is compromise. You give a little sometimes, you give a lot sometimes and she will do the same. You are only fooling yourself if you believe that marriage is a fifty-fifty partnership. It's more like a seventy-thirty or even an eighty-twenty. Neither of you should have to cave in to the other's demands all of the time, but if you both want the relationship to work, you will have to be willing to be the one who compromises some of the time.

Oh Queen, Reign Forever

I have been asked if this process of compromising is intended to place a man in a slave-master position with his wife. A Total Man is not a slave to any woman. He freely chooses to give in to his wife's desires even though he may not always want to. She, in turn, will be grateful for his willingness to meet her more than half way and will respond in kind.

Marriage has often been compared to a monarchy. Think about the current sovereignty in England. Queen Elizabeth's decisions are final. She has a husband to help her to make decisions, but when they disagree, the queen's word is still law. She sits on the throne and has the right, no, the responsibility to express her views. When the prince sits by her side, she probably relies on his good judgement, but if there is ever a difference of opinion, it is the queen who makes the decisions.

Hold on a minute, I know what you're thinking. "What if the queen makes the wrong decision," you're asking yourself. "If I know she's making a mistake, am I supposed to sit quietly at her side and let her mess up?" The answer is an unqualified "Yes!" Keep in mind that you will make mistakes too and she, as a good and gracious queen, should accept your decisions and not throw your poor judgement into your face. You must give her this same courtesy. She is an adult and knows full well that she must live with the consequences of every choice she makes.

In many marriages today, the husband believes that his word is law. If this works for you and your spouse, fine. In other marriages the "queen" and "king" rule side by side. One never makes a decision without the other. Again, if you and your spouse are comfortable with this arrangement, stick with it. Most marriages are a matter of give and take. Sometimes you will be the leader and make the final decision, other times your wife will make the decisions and you must abide by them. Let me remind you one more time—the key word is COMPROMISE. Try it and see how well it works!

I know you are probably having serious doubts about now. No one has ever expected you to give in before. I used to have the same attitude, but I changed mine and so can you. No woman wants a man who tries to dominate her all of the time, but she doesn't want one who is a doormat, either. She wants one who states his opinions in a calm and reasonable manner, who is not afraid to admit when he is wrong.

Wedding Bell Blues

Last year my wife made plans to attend her best friend's wedding, which happened to be on Super Bowl Sunday. I wanted to watch the game on our big screen television more than you can possibly imagine (especially since I had a hundred dollars riding on San Francisco to win). My wife expected me to go with her. The wedding had been planned for months and she was, after all, the matron of honor. I finally decided to go with her and tape the game on the VCR. She knew what a sacrifice I was making and treated me with tenderness the entire day. I did wonder why she didn't tell me to stay home and watch the game. She knew how much it meant to me, but I know I made the right decision and the reward was well worth missing one game (yes, even the Super Bowl!).

A few months later, we disagreed about what to do on our upcoming vacation. She wanted to spend a week in New York and I wanted to go fishing in the mountains. We discussed both options, but it was obvious that we could only do one of them together and we did want to spend the time with each other. I finally agreed to abide by her decision and knew that I would have a good time in the Big Apple. Much to my surprise she came in from work the next day wearing a fishing hat and carrying a new rod and reel. "Mountains, here we come," she announced with a big grin.

Compromising is not always this easy. I don't want to give you the impression that I am being unrealistic, so I'd like to share a stupid personal experience with you. I'm not proud of myself, but I did it.

On another vacation, friends invited us to spend the day sightseeing with them. I didn't want to. I wanted to spend the day in a lounge chair by the hotel pool catching up on my reading. My wife asked that I accompany them and I adamantly refused. "I'm not going to go without you," she said. "They invited both of us and I don't want to have to make excuses for you. You can always read tomorrow." I wouldn't budge. My wife was practically begging me to go on a date with her and I refused.

I won. We didn't go sightseeing, but I didn't enjoy my book. I felt so guilty for acting like a spoiled brat that I couldn't relax at all. Worst of all, she wouldn't talk to me for the rest of the vacation. I apologized for my stupidity later, but she needed time to recover from her hurt feelings. I know I felt worse than she did and I learned my lesson. Having your own way is not worth having a tense relationship with the woman you love.

Modifying my behavior to meet her needs is not always easy, but it's often the right thing to do. And I know that when I don't want to compromise, it's my problem, not hers. Sometimes I tell my wife, "You think you're right, but in my opinion, I'm right. We may not always agree, but I need to tell you how I feel about things." Seeing things from her viewpoint helps me to understand how she feels. Sometimes I have to struggle to make myself agree to compromise, but the rewards I reap are always worth the extra effort. When my wife snuggles in my arms at the end of a long day, it makes everything worthwhile.

Rockers Away

Denise and Ron had been married for ten years. Their first five years were a financial nightmare, but Debbie was finally promoted to CEO of her company and their lifestyle seemed to change overnight. They bought a new house. Denise thought they would be able to entertain more often, but Ron was really a loner and didn't look forward to a house full of guests night after night. When Denise began to plan her first large dinner party, Ron refused to help.

Ron is now divorced. He still lives in the lovely home purchased with Denise's money and Denise lives in a gorgeous townhouse in North Dallas with her new friend who shares her enthusiasm for entertaining. In marriage it makes sense for both of you to jog in the same direction. Otherwise one of you will get lost and end up making the rest of the trip alone.

David, a handsome executive, was married to Rochelle, an antique collector who loved to spend her weekends in the country, hunting for new pieces for their home. David had never cared for old things and always stayed home when Rochelle made her weekly excursions. One night in class, he announced that he "couldn't stand those stuffy barns and auction houses," but he planned to go with Rochelle next weekend, "because I know how much she enjoys those trips."

That night, instead of sitting on the couch with the remote in his fist, he joined Rochelle in the garage to keep her company as she stripped the old varnish off of a deacon's bench. While she worked diligently, he didn't say much, but stayed with her. The next day Rochelle came home with what she said was "the best news." Ron thought she had decided to give up antiquing, or, at the very least, had found out she was finally pregnant. Instead she announced with a big smile on her face that she had "just heard about the biggest antique sale in the state. It's being held in

West Texas next weekend!"

Summer arrived and I heard less and less from David. I worried about him and wondered how he was fairing. One day a beautiful post-card arrived from Phoenix. It read:

So far the Total Man has survived trips to antique malls in Houston, Abilene and now Phoenix. I am up and ready to go with a smile on my face every Saturday morning by six o'clock. Yesterday I found the nicest rocking chair and bought it for pennies. This Total Man has become an antique nut thanks to his charming wife!

Yes, I Want To Go Too!

Has your wife ever come to you full of enthusiasm and suggested what she thought was an exciting idea and you responded with, "Okay, but..." It may have been a simple request like, "Let's go to the movies this evening," but you effectively dampened her eagerness by saying, "Okay, but." You stomped on her idea with your negativity. It doesn't matter what her idea was or what reason you gave for not wanting to participate. It had the same effect as challenging her decisions. She couldn't persuade you to join her and she resented you.

You may not realize how often you argue with her. In fact, she may be making plans without you all of the time because of this very reason. The next time she asks you if you want to accompany her somewhere, respond with "Yes, I want to go too!" You may have to revive her with a damp washcloth, but she will love having your company when she comes to. All of her suggestions won't appeal to you (maybe none of them will), but try them anyway. You may find that you actually enjoy some of the activities. If a friend had made the same suggestion, you would have probably responded positively without giving it a second thought. Can you do any less for the woman you love?

On many vacations, my wife and I have had endless arguments about where to eat. I'm a meat and potatoes kind of guy and she prefers oriental cuisine (anything with lots of vegetables in it really appeals to her). When we didn't go where I wanted to eat I've been so upset that I couldn't enjoy the meal. I carried packets of antacids with me wherever we went. I finally learned that my belief that I had a "right" to select every restaurant we ate in was causing us both indigestion, and it wasn't worth it. Everything is so much simpler when I state my preference and we make a joint decision. Sometimes we eat where I want and sometimes we eat where she wants.

I try to remember to tell my wife, "The decision is yours. We can do whatever you want." When I trust her judgement I find that she does not take advantage of the situation. She is much more willing to compromise and let me do what I want more than half the time. She is grateful for the freedom of choice so she does not act like an ogre. She weighs the decisions, whether they are about where to eat or where to live, and often asks my opinion. When she makes a decision that I don't like, I don't argue. The lines of communication have been opened and I know that we will discuss each situation as it arises.

After I made the assignment to my class to adapt to their wives' lifestyles, John, a Houston husband, drove home, anxious to put the plan into action. He stopped at a local restaurant and picked up his wife's favorite dinner of vegetable lasagna and Caesar salad. He planned to set the table with real dishes instead of paper and even use cloth napkins. He soon found out that the most elaborately laid plans don't always work out.

John pulled his favorite cotton shirt out of the hamper and hung it on the back of the bathroom door, hoping that some of the wrinkles would come out when the room filled with steam from his shower. Just as he stepped under the spray of hot water, he heard his wife come through the front door. What was she doing home at five o'clock? He started to scream out in frustration, but caught himself just in time. He was determined to adapt to her schedule. When he had jumped out of the shower and donned his clothes, even though he hadn't dried completely, he rushed to the kitchen only to find her eating a hastily made sandwich while leaning against the cabinet. "Hi," she said around a mouthful of bread and cheese. "I can't stay. We're having a big production meeting at the office tonight and I don't think I'll be home before midnight."

At the next meeting, John expressed his frustration. "I was so pissed off," he said. "But, I didn't let her know. I silently called the Total Man class every rotten name I could think of, but I walked her to the door and promised myself that I'd give this thing one more try. I wanted to keep a good attitude so I gave her a hug and told her to be careful. I told her that I'd wait up for her. I was shocked when she came back through the door at nine-thirty and told me the meeting had been cut short. We had a wonderful time together."

Keep The Fire Burning

At a recent opening at our local art gallery, I overheard one husband say to another, "I know how much your wife admires Monet—are you a big fan of his too?" The other husband smiled and shook his head. "No," he responded, "But I love my wife."

I admit to spending a lot of time listening to other people's conversations, but I learn a lot from them. Men who complain that the sizzle has gone out of their marriages have no one to blame but themselves. If a man wants to keep the romance alive, he must work at it. If his wife is forced to consistently attend the art shows or the ballet or even open house at school alone, is there any reason to expect her to want to jump into bed with the man who ignores her needs and desires? A good sex life starts hours before bedtime and takes a whole lot of effort, but isn't it worth it?

It is only when a man decides to become a part of his wife's life that he becomes really attractive to her. He becomes a commodity that she cannot do without. He becomes her king!

8

Appreciate Her

I joined my wife when she attended a recent conference in California. One evening before dinner, we stopped to talk with a doctor she had been acquainted with for years. For some reason, the conversation turned to the doctor's partner, who had died two years before. "She was the most amazing person I ever knew," she said. "She was only forty-five when she died. Not long before she died, she shared some of her personal thoughts about life with me. She said, `As you get older you will find that the thing you treasure in life above everything else is loyalty, and the hardest thing to accept is ingratitude.'"

The most treasured quality in another human being: loyalty. The thing most difficult to accept: ingratitude. As I thought about the doctor's words, I realized that the two qualities were almost opposites. This well-loved doctor must have felt the hurt of ingratitude more than once.

Uncaring or Overreacting

Wives also feel that deep hurt. One told me, "Maybe I'm just overly sensitive, but people tend to be so unappreciative nowadays. Everybody expects to get something for nothing, and my husband is the worst one of all. I get no pleasure out of doing things for him because he never shows any gratitude." An ungrateful husband is no joy to his wife. So many men have forgotten those two little words, "Thank you." They expect their wives to do so many things for them, like cook and clean and care for the children while at the same time holding a full-time job outside of the home. How difficult could it be for them to let her know how much they appreciate her efforts?

If your wife came through the door tonight with a six-pack of your favorite beer, would you be grateful or would you wonder what she was up to? I think many husbands do not express appreciation, but would automatically react in one of the following ways:

1. He'd say, "Now what?"

Translation: "You're being nice to me. You must want something."
His wife instantly picks up on the unspoken accusation. She suddenly
feels guilty, even though she was only trying to be nice and didn't want
anything at all.

2. Or he'd say, "I can't believe you actually remembered what I like
to drink!"

Translation: "I've been telling you what I like for years. It's about
time you remembered! I work hard and I deserve to have exactly what I
want." The wife has witnessed a transformation right before her eyes.
The husband has suddenly become a creditor to whom she has owed the
right kind of beer for years.

3. Another might say, "Was the grocery store having a clearance
sale?"

Translation: "The amount you spent on this gift directly reflects how
much you love me. I'd really love you if you had bought me a case, but
I can't get too excited over a six-pack." The stunned wife now views her
husband as the cashier in the grocery store who glares at her with disdain
because she's so cheap she will only purchase the dented cans from the
discount bin.

4. Finally, he might unenthusiastically say, "Oh, beer, how nice."

Translation: "This is exactly what I don't need. Didn't I tell you yesterday that I was trying to lose ten pounds? How am supposed to resist
the temptation of cold beer? Don't you want my diet to be successful?"
The wife is now staring at her husband in disbelief. Everything she does
for him is wrong. She is totally incapable of giving him what he wants.

More often than not, a husband reacts in one of these ways, all of
which are prime examples of shameless ingratitude. Once in awhile,
however, there is the husband who overreacts to everything his wife
does. He will smile and gush for hours over the simplest things: "Oh,
honey, I can't believe you brought me some beer. You are so sweet. I
appreciate you so much." And on and on until the poor wife just wants to
scream.

This overreacting doesn't fool anyone, especially the wife. She's
heard the same silly reaction over and over. The reaction is always the
same no matter what the wife does or the reason behind her action. This
is still ingratitude, only couched in different words. The wife knows her
husband doesn't believe she deserves an honest response for her efforts.

Level of Recognition

Stop for a moment and consider your level of recognition for all the things your wife does for you. Are you guilty of that disgusting act of ingratitude? Do you recognize how much effort she puts in to providing for you? Not just the extras, but the money she provides for groceries, clothing and those Sunday golf games you cannot live without?

Recognition involves two parts—internal and external. A husband will never feel gratitude if he has the mistaken idea that he deserves to be taken to dinner and a movie once a week. He must learn to understand that the effort his wife makes to provide him with treats is a privilege, and not his God-given right as a man. He must learn to appreciate, and to express his appreciation, for the things his wife does for him.

Secondly, inward appreciation must be expressed outwardly. Your wife doesn't know you are grateful if you do not show her or tell her. If she cooks dinner, you can clear the table and load the dishwasher. If she brings home dessert, you can serve it, along with a cup of her favorite coffee. Show her that you recognize and appreciate all that she does for you.

Thank her verbally. Tell her out loud how much you appreciate what she does. Your words may elicit an unexpected response; she will probably start expressing her gratitude for your efforts too! Kindness almost always breeds kindness.

I recently witnessed a woman shopping for a birthday gift for her husband (yes, I was eavesdropping again). She told the salesman, "Just give me a box of golf balls. It doesn't matter what I buy because he'll return it anyway." Then she smiled as she said, "My assistant's birthday is coming up soon. I'd like to buy something special for him. I love to watch the expression on his face when I hand him a gift." She spent twice the amount of time picking out the gift for her grateful assistant.

When a woman gives her husband a gift, the only reward she is looking for is his pleasure. One woman presented her husband with a new bowling ball, but he let her know that it wasn't the brand he would have chosen himself. He took away her happiness by constantly grumbling about the quality of her gift. He finally exchanged it for the ball that he wanted. His wife hasn't brought home any gifts since. Why would she?

You may not be crazy over every gift you receive, but be careful with your response. If at all possible, use it anyway. Remember when you bought her the gallon of perfume for $9.99 at the discount pharmacy? She was happy that you thought of her even though the perfume burned her skin every time she put it on and you finally threw it out with the rest of the trash.

Let your wife know how much you appreciate her taking the time out of her busy schedule to purchase the gift. If you really don't like the gift, don't lie and say that you do. You're wife always knows when you're lying and she will become aggravated. Do make sure you tell her that you recognize her thoughtfulness and you really appreciate the surprise.

My wife recently took my daughter and two of her friends to the mall. When they got out of the car, they all expressed their thanks and my daughter bent into the open window and kissed her mother's cheek. My wife felt like a queen all day. Child-like appreciation always lifts the heart. Women need that too!

The perfect balance between uncaring indifference and overreacting is a grateful level of recognition for the time and effort another person puts into doing things for you simply because she wants to. A simple "Thank you" will do more to lift your wife's spirits than you can possibly know. The next time she does something for you, let her know that you understand she did it because she wanted to. You'll be pleased at how often she will go out of her way to do the little, unexpected things just to please you.

Lesson Number 2

1. Accept your wife just as she is. Write out two lists—one of her faults (if any) and one of her virtues. Take a long, hard look at her faults and then throw this small slip of paper directly into the trash. Focus on her virtues. Carry that list in your wallet and refer to it whenever you are feeling depressed or angry.

2. Admire your wife on a daily basis. If you actually find it necessary, you may refer to your list. Say something nice about her mind today. Let her know how proud you are of her abilities.

3. Adapt to her lifestyle. Accept her friends, hectic schedule, and lifestyle as your own. Ask her to write down the top three changes she would like to see take place in your household. Read the list, study it, know it, and most of all—do it. Once you have mastered all of these changes, approach your wife with a smile on your face and ask her if there is anything else she wants changed. If there is, do that too.

4. Appreciate all that she does for you. Sincerely tell her "thank you" with your attitudes, actions and words. Give her your undivided attention, and try not to play "channel-surf" with the remote control after she comes home.

Part Four

SEX 101

9

Waxing The Car

Let's start by going back to the time you first met the woman who is now your wife. Let's focus on the first time she met you. Remember how much time you took making sure you looked good before you went to pick her up? Remember how you used to take a shower and shave every day, how you kept your hair neatly trimmed and used just a touch of aftershave? You were so happy and confident. You could hardly wait to see her. It gave you a little thrill to watch her come down the sidewalk toward your car, knowing how much she wanted to be with you.

Now let's focus on the present. What did you look like last night when she came home from work? What did you have on this morning when she left the house? Guys, let's face it, is it any wonder that the honeymoon is over? Can you blame her if she no longer finds you the most desirable thing in the world?

It doesn't have to be like this. Keep in mind that you are the man she wants to come home to at the end of the day. She chose you out of all the other men she knew. You are still the one who can turn her on anytime you make the effort.

Boring To Wow

Your wife does not expect, or want, you to look like an eighteen-year-old boy, but she does want you to take care of yourself. The outer shell of yours is much like a car on a dealership lot. It may have a nice engine under the hood and drive like a dream, but not many people are going to find it appealing if it's been allowed to become rusty and dirty. Does your exterior shine as much as it did four or five years ago?

Is the last view your wife has of you, as she rushes out the door in the morning, one of you slumped down on the couch in your tattered t-shirt and boxer shorts, clutching a cup of coffee in one hand and the sports page in the other?

Have you been neglecting your mind as much as you have your body? There is nothing more appealing to a woman than an intelligent man who can participate in a conversation. Yes, women appreciate a man who looks nice, but nothing turns her on more than a man who keeps his mind active. Start reading something other than the sports page. Watch the news on a daily basis. Let her know that you are interested in what is taking place in the world around you.

Let's face it, most women are different from men. Sure, she appreciates a flat stomach or a nice set of biceps, but the most important thing to her is a man who can stimulate her mind. Women are much more forgiving than we are when it comes to physical attractiveness, but they are less likely to accept a man who bores them just because he has a nice body. Why not spend a little more time catching up on current events and a little less time worrying about whether your favorite basketball team will make the playoffs this year?

Welcome Home

Take a few extra minutes this afternoon to take a shower before your wife gets home. She appreciates the fact that you gave the dog a bath, mowed the lawn and changed the oil in your car, but she doesn't want to smell it.

If you have children, try to find an evening babysitter at least one night a week. It's difficult for your wife to feel romantic when she comes through the door and the kids jump all over her, trying to out-shout one another so they can be the first to tell her what the other one did wrong. Make the evening totally relaxing for both of you.

Variety adds Spice

Recently I was invited to give a short lecture at a weekly meeting for a local women's group. My topic was to be "The Changing Role for Men in the '90s." I was used to public speaking; however standing up in front of a group made up entirely of women seemed a little intimidating—but I thought I should give it a try and I'm glad I did.

My speech took about ten minutes and was followed by a brief question and answer period. The women seemed to be appreciative and applauded politely when I finished. I left the podium and took a seat against the wall where I thought I would be less conspicuous.

A young woman took my place at the front of the room, glanced nervously in my direction, and then announced that she would "like to continue with last week's topic on sex." A few women in the audience tittered nervously, but the discussion soon became very intense and everyone seemed to forget that I was there. I learned some things that night that I would like to share with you.

1. Affectionate behavior does not always have to lead to sex. One woman bitterly complained that she had gotten to the point where she no longer wanted to hug or kiss her husband because he always assumed that any affection she displayed toward him meant they had to jump into bed. Women crave affection as much as we do, but they need to know that you care about them outside of the bedroom as well as inside. Give her little hugs and kisses throughout the day just to let her know that you are thinking about her, not because you're interested in an afternoon "quickie."

2. Lovemaking is not a race. The man who finishes the fastest is not the winner. Take your time. You may be aroused and raring to go after a few kisses, but, more than likely, your wife is not. Slow down. Relax. Take the time to make sure your wife is as aroused as you are.

3. If you don't know, ask. If you are not sure what your wife likes—and let's be honest here, many of us don't know—ask. Does she enjoy you nibbling on her ears, or does it simply tickle? The easiest way to make sure that you are doing the right things is to ask questions. If there is something that she doesn't like, or something that she does like that you haven't been doing, don't take it as a personal insult when she lets you know. Pay attention to what she tells you. If you are willing to please her, it is almost certain that she will want to do more things to please you too.

4. Let your wife seduce you. It is not an affront to your masculinity if your wife wants to be the aggressor once in awhile. Keep in mind, however, that being seduced does not mean that you lie back and let her do everything. Get involved. You don't want her to lie there and stare at the ceiling the whole time, and she doesn't want that from you, either. Let her know how much you enjoy what she is doing.

5. Routine is boring. One wife said that every time she and her husband made love, he did the exact same things. The same number of kisses each time, a few squeezes and rubs here and there—never any variety, and that was what she craved more than anything. Surprise her! Start out the evening with a foot massage, nibble on her toes if she enjoys that.

Join her in a long bubble bath or a hot shower. If she likes poetry, read
her some love poems, or write your own. You may feel silly, but she will
appreciate the effort. If she enjoys classical music, even if you don't,
spend an hour or so listening with her. It may sound trite, but variety is
the spice of life (and love). Don't become so set in your ways that your
spouse becomes bored with you.

The key to a satisfying sex life is knowing your partner. If you both
enjoy playing "dress up" once in awhile—do it. If you both enjoy making love outdoors, that's okay too, just make sure you choose a location
that offers total privacy. If you both only enjoy making love every third
Thursday when the moon is full... you get my point. I also hope that you
have noticed the emphasis I have put on the word both. Never, ever
expect your partner to do anything that makes her unhappy or uncom-
fortable. If you are considerate of her feelings, she will be considerate of
yours!

10

Bumps In The Bedsprings

Sex is the one subject we all seem to be obsessed with. Magazines are full of articles telling us how to improve our sex lives; nightly soap operas, where the characters hop from bed to bed, dominate television entertainment. If we are interested in the sexual habits of our favorite stars, we can watch gossip TV to find out who is sleeping with whom and where. How-to books dominate the shelves of our favorite bookstores and advice radio programs fill the airwaves. Sex is no longer a forbidden topic that people whisper about secretly.

Why are so many men having more sex, but enjoying it less? What has happened to the fun in sex?

A prominent divorce lawyer once stated that nine times out of ten, divorce started in the bedroom. Many of us did not believe her at the time, but survey after survey has shown that when a marriage becomes bumpy, the bumps are usually in the bedsprings. In other words, if a couple has a satisfying sex life, they will be a lot more determined to work out their problems in order to save the marriage.

One such bump in the bedsprings is the sexless marriage. I heard one man say, "We can't have sex because our teenage son's room is right next to ours and the headboard continually hits the wall. He would know what we were doing!" I wondered how long it has been for them. I also wondered why they didn't fix the headboard or move the bed, but that's another topic. This incident is not as unusual as it may seem. I know of many married couples who go without sex for weeks and months on end. The excuses are many and varied, but the results are usually disastrous. Sex should not be the basis for a marriage, but a good marriage should include a sex life that is satisfactory to both partners.

Well-known advice columnist, Ann Landers, received a letter[3] from a man who claimed that his wife was a nice person whom he liked, but he had gotten to the point where he just wanted to be her friend. He claimed that he didn't want to bother with sex anymore.

"There is no one else in my life, in case you are interested. There is nothing wrong with my wife and we don't fight. I just find that the whole sex thing is over-rated and I don't care anymore." He wanted to know if his way of thinking was all right.

Ann wrote back, "It's fine with ME—the question is whether or not it's okay with your wife. If she is in agreement, then you have no problem. The trouble starts when there is a difference of opinion."3

I believe many men feel this way. They would like to forego sex and keep "playing" at marriage. A fulfilling sex life takes effort on the part of both people involved, but it is well worth the effort.

Where is the Thrill?

A young husband confessed, "I get a thrill out of sex, but my wife never seems to enjoy it. We've been married for five years and I don't think she's ever had an orgasm."

Many men mistakenly believe that sex in marriage is simply doing what comes naturally. If things don't happen naturally, their wives are disappointed and so are the men. She begins to develop an "I don't care" attitude and loses interest. We husbands misinterpret her feelings and believe she doesn't care about us. This is a sad state. A married woman should not have to go around feeling unfulfilled. A Total Man knows that sex is essential for a happy marriage. Unless he and his wife are both thrilled by their sex life, his marriage rates only a B- at best.

Sex should not simply be the joining of a man's and woman's sex organs. It is meant to be so much more. The Old English term for sexual intercourse is "to know." A man and woman should know each other in every sense of the word.

The sexual climax is the greatest physical pleasure known to woman (and man). Research reveals that climax rejuvenates the body and the mind. It also relieves stress, headaches and, in some cases, menstrual cramps. A satisfying sex life also promotes emotional well being.

If the woman is not being fulfilled, it is up to the couple to discover what the problem is, and to do everything in their power to correct it. A man should never assume that there is "something wrong with her." If one partner is left feeling empty and frustrated, it is not her worry. The concern belongs to both partners and they should work together to reach a solution. There could be a physical reason as to why sex is not enjoyable for her—visit a physician together if you suspect this may be true. Don't think the problem will correct itself—it won't! Work together to discover what the cause of the difficulties is and then work together to rectify things.

In The Garden

In the beginning, God created man, who lived alone in the garden. The days were long, and the nights were longer. There was no one to give him emotional support or encourage him when he was feeling down. God saw how lonely man was, so he presented him with woman as a partner, the best thing any man could ever hope for.

God performed the first surgery there in the garden. He took a rib from the man's side and created woman as man's instant companion. When the man woke up from the anesthesia, he rubbed his eyes sleepily and stared at this fascinating new creature in wonder and awe. "Where have you been hiding?" he muttered. "I thought I knew every inch of this place." (According to Genesis 2:23, what he actually said was, "This is now bone of my bone, and flesh of my flesh.")

The first man was intelligent enough to know that woman was exactly what he needed in order to survive in the world. God told the new couple to "go forth and multiply," (Genesis 1:28). The "newlyweds," Adam and Eve, had the responsibility of populating the earth, but God knew that they would not get very far if sex was not enjoyable. He, therefore, made sex to fulfill two purposes, one—to supply the world with children, and two—to bring great pleasure and joy to both the woman and the man.

God felt no need to supply Adam and Eve with guidelines or how-to manuals. He knew that they loved each other enough to learn together. Each would find great joy in making the other happy. God's first man was an unselfish lover; he knew that half the pleasure of sex was in making sure that his woman was satisfied. God, and his new creations, knew that what he had done was GOOD!

Yes, Her Too!

If you and your partner are not enjoying a satisfying sex life, it is up to you to change it. It might be that you need a change of attitude, but that is a possible goal to reach. The number of husbands who are ignorant of their wives' sexual needs is astonishing. In class, one husband learned for the first time that his wife should also experience an orgasm. He went home and shared this news with his wife (who, I'm sure looked at him like he was a Total Idiot!). "I always thought only bad women did," he had mumbled. In this case total re-education of the husband was in order. He reported that most of the tension around the house seemed to disappear like magic once his wife started receiving sexual satisfaction. Another surprise!

We men tend to think of ourselves as real studs who could satisfy any woman at any time, but if we are honest we will admit that there are many of us who don't know what the hell we are supposed to be doing. What's even worse is that some of us don't really care.

As I mentioned earlier, there are many how-to books available on the market today that may help you. Another good way to get to the root of the problem is to communicate with your wife. Sit down, at a time when you are both relaxed, preferably outside of the bedroom when you are both fully clothed, and have a heart to heart talk with her. There may be a simple solution. If not, you may want to seek professional help. Your inability to understand your wife's needs may have a deep-seated cause. There is nothing to be ashamed of if you do decide to seek the advice of a professional. It takes a big man to admit that he needs help. Remember, you are not just doing this for your wife, you are doing it for the sake of the marriage that you both treasure.

One more thing to keep in mind is the fact that not all sexual problems begin in the bedroom. We all know that couples should not use sex as a weapon, but we realistically know it happens. You're wife may have some good reasons as to why she no longer enjoys sex with you. Are you doing your share of the housework, the shopping, the childcare (No, you are not helping her out if you watch the kids for a few hours. They are your children too and she should not have to shoulder the entire burden of caring for them), and the myriad other chores that she takes care of on a daily basis? Be honest. If you are not participating in the responsibilities of the marriage, it is time to change your attitude. Being a Total Man means sharing all of the duties. A simple change in attitude may be all it takes to make your sex life sizzle instead of fizzle!

Passing On The Fallacy

Today, even with all our advanced technology, men are still passing on their misconceptions about sex to their sons. "Women really don't care about sex. It's just something they do to please us." Wake up, guys!

Sex is meant to be pleasurable for women as well as for men. If we don't start teaching our sons the truth, they may grow up to be unhappy, dissatisfied men. If we guide our sons and teach them the facts, they will be happier adults. Do not consider sex as a taboo subject. Be realistic. In this day and age, kids see more action on television than we ever thought possible. Your son already knows about the birds and the bees; he needs you to teach him right from wrong and fact from fiction.

It should not only be your responsibility to teach him about birth control and sexually transmitted diseases—it should also be your responsibility to inform him of the facts. He deserves to know that women enjoy sex as much as men do, and he needs to learn to respect women both in and out of the bedroom.

Come on, dads! What are you waiting for?

Resent Not

Resentment in a marriage does not necessarily mean one or another of the partners is at fault. A woman may feel an unconscious resentment toward all men because her father ignored her when she was a little girl. She saw how much time he spent with her brothers and she wanted his attention too. It broke her heart to think that he cared for them more than he did for her and she subconsciously makes her husband pay for the mistakes made by another man.

A man may feel resentful toward women in general because he does not understand them. He has been socialized to believe that women are of a different species and has always felt that he has had to walk on tiptoes around them so as not to cause offense. He doesn't know how to express his concerns to his wife and he resents the differences he has been conditioned to perceive.

Hidden resentments can be the death of a marriage. The old axiom, "Honesty is the best policy," still rings true. Talk to your wife, let her know how you feel. It is not shameful to admit that you have fears and doubts. Remember, she does too. Maybe you can help each other work through your problems. If they are deep-seated problems, therapy may be in order and that's okay too. Emotional stability and happiness leads to stronger marriages.

Do not use sex as a weapon. This can only destroy the relationship. If there is a problem, sit down and talk it out. Silent anger doesn't solve anything. It only leads to more resentment.

My friend, Ted, did not see much of his wife on the weekends. She took a sculpting class and played on a company-sponsored softball team. Ted punished her by refusing to make love.

In class, Ted came to realize that his wife needs to have outside interests and other friends, just like he does. He also learned that his wife will not make an effort to meet his needs if he "punishes" her. The next time Ted's wife left for her class, he said, "Have fun, honey." He felt his resentment rising, but he pushed it back down and smiled as she went out the door.

To his surprise, she came home early that afternoon. The instructor had urged her to stay for an additional class, but she refused. When questioned, she had simply responded, "I want to go home and spend some quality time with my husband." This woman realized that her husband was making an effort to meet her needs and she was more willing to meet his.

These problems demonstrate just how far from the bedroom sexual problems can originate. I urge you to work through your resentments once and for all. A satisfying sex life is essential for a good marriage. With an honest effort on the part of both spouses, it is possible!

Can You Forgive and Forget?

Two years ago my friend Bill discovered that his wife was having an affair with her boss. Bill was devastated. He loved his wife and could not understand why she felt the need to turn to another man for sexual satisfaction.

Bill's first instinct was to angrily confront his wife and demand that she put an end to the affair immediately. If she did not, he would leave her and do everything in his power to gain custody of their three children. Bill, however, was a very astute man, and knew that if he gave his wife an ultimatum, she would pack up and leave. Did he really want to lose the woman he had lived with and loved for the past ten years? Did he want to put his children through the heartache of divorce and separation from one of their parents? He knew he had to talk to his wife and find out what had happened to cause her to turn away from him.

That evening, after the children had been bathed and tucked into their beds, Bill asked his wife to join him at the kitchen table. He poured two cups of coffee, and began hesitantly, "Honey, I know you're having an affair." His wife promptly burst into tears and admitted her guilt. "Why?" he asked.

She explained to Bill that it wasn't the sex so much as needing someone to talk to, someone who thought what she had to say was important and who really listened when she had a contribution to make. "But I listen to you." Bill replied.

"No, you don't. You tune me out all of the time. I try to tell you about my day and you mumble something or other from behind the sports page. I need someone who finds me interesting and cares about what I care about. You just don't care anymore."

By this time, Bill was nearly in tears himself. "I love you more than anything else in the world," he said. "You and the kids are the most important things in my life and I don't want to lose you."

His wife smiled through her tears. "Do you know how long it has been since you said those words to me? I love you, Bill. I really do. Can you ever forgive me?"

Bill promised to try. He admits that it hasn't been easy, but he is working at it. When his wife calls to say she is working late, he often suffers through a moment of doubt, but he knows that if he does not learn to trust her again the marriage is over.

"An affair," Bill told me, "Is usually not the problem with the marriage. It is a symptom of something else. I let my wife believe that I no longer needed her or cared about her and she went searching for someone who did. I forgave her a long time ago. Yes, she was the one who fooled around, but it wasn't all her fault. I neglected her and forgot my marriage vows, to love, honor and cherish; I didn't cherish her anymore and that's what she needed. Forgetting is the hard part. But I keep trying and that's what it takes."

Bill is a very understanding man, more so than most of us. He realized that the problems he and his wife had were caused by a lack of communication on both their parts. He had become so wrapped up in his own little world that he neglected the people who needed him the most.

Can you forgive and forget? Marriage comes with no guarantees. There will be problems and both partners will make mistakes. Can you accept a sincere apology and a promise to try harder? Forgiving means that you will not harbor resentment against your partner for past mistakes. Let them stay in the past. Forgetting means just that. Don't bring up past failures every time a new problem arises. Know that your wife loves you and she is as determined as you are to make your marriage work. It is time to move on to better things.

Fireworks In The Morning/Fireworks At Night

I mentioned in an earlier section that a woman needs a man who can stimulate her mind. This is worth further discussion. Please note that her most important sex organ is not what lies between her legs (as many of you think), it is what lies between her ears. No man, no matter how wonderful he thinks he is, can turn on a woman who does not want to be turned on.

Unless you take the time to know your wife as an intelligent woman, you will never know her in bed. She needs to be told, and shown, that you respect her intelligence and rely on her to help you function as a Total Man. Let her know that her opinions and ideas are important to you. Make sure she understands that you do not view her as only a body, there to fulfill your physical needs. A woman who knows her man values her as a thinking human being will allow herself to be aroused by you and you alone.

Your wife needs, and deserves, a warm, caring partner in bed. If you are a stingy lover, chances are high that she will be too. Satisfy her by giving her everything she wants, and she will want to do the same for you.

It may take some time for you to reach the closeness you yearn for with your wife, but don't give up. With the right attitude, things will improve. You may not give up all of your bad habits and misconceptions overnight, but in time you will. Your mental attitude will bring about physical changes in both of you. That's when the fireworks will start!

11

Sensational Sex

Sex is fifteen minutes in bed at midnight; sensational sex is the climax of an atmosphere that has been carefully set all day. Your attitude during your wife's first ten waking minutes in the morning sets the tone for her entire day. You can set the atmosphere for love even before breakfast. Keep your hands to yourself when you first wake up. Brush your teeth and shave before she gets out of bed. Make sure to wipe out the sink and flush the toilet. Have the coffee ready for her for a change and bring the newspaper in from the front yard.

Remember, she can stand almost anything but boredom. The same old boxer shorts and the grease-stained tee shirt with the big whole in the armpit month after month are not too enticing. Treat her and yourself to some new pajamas and leave the old sweatsocks in the hamper.

One husband actually changed the sheets while his wife was dressing for work. As she gazed at him in astonishment, he held up the soiled linens and whispered, "I'll have these washed, dried, folded, and put away before you get home tonight." If you expect great sex tonight, it should definitely start in the morning, with a sincere display of assistance in the housework department. That's basic. Sex 101.

Tomorrow morning as your wife leaves for the office, stand at the door and wave until she's out of sight, then run like hell to catch the bus on the corner so that you're not late for your own job.

In class recently, one hunky guy I'll call Alec told how he had anxiously anticipated his wife's homecoming one evening. At five o'clock he called her office a little nervously and said, "Sweetheart, I'm anxiously waiting for you to come home. I really want you."

Denise, his wife, made no reply.

He breathed heavily into the phone. "Is there someone there with you, honey?"

Again, no response.

He assumed that she must be pre-occupied. "Well, I'll be waiting."

They both hung up.

A few minutes later the phone rang. It was Denise. "My secretary said you just called to tell me you wanted something. Whatever it is, it'll have to wait. I've got a late meeting. You'll have to order take-out."

The sequel to the story was even worse. Alec called his pal, Jake, to tell him what had happened. Jake couldn't wait to try it on his wife to see if he could order take-out too. He called her office and when a female voice answered, he blurted out, "Baby, hurry home! I want your body now!"

The voice on the other end demanded, "Who is this? If you call here again, you creep, I'll call the police!" Jake realized that another woman had answered the phone and quickly hung up. He prayed that his wife's office didn't have "star-69" and would be unable to call back and identify him.

That night when his wife came through the front door, she said, "You won't believe what happened today. Marcie got an obscene phone call at the office!" (He never told her, by the way, who the obscene caller was.)

So when you call your wife's office be sure you've got the right woman. Then keep it short, after all she is a busy woman. In fact, if it's not an emergency, wait until she gets home. You know her boss frowns on personal calls during business hours.

Noontime Delight

If you pack your wife's lunch in the morning, try tucking in a surprise love note. Have a tasteful bouquet of flowers delivered to her desk even though it's not your anniversary or her birthday. Or appear in person. Even if she asks you to leave because you're interrupting an important luncheon with her biggest out-of-state client, she'll know that you cared. She'll also know that you forgot, even though she's been telling you how nervous she was about this meeting for the last two weeks.

Arrange your day's activities so that you'll be totally and eagerly prepared as she walks in the door. A psychiatrist told me, "Most women would be less preoccupied if they could come home once in a while and find the breakfast dishes done and the laundry started. It could be the most relaxing part of the day."

I find that after a hard day at the office most wives don't want to rush around cooking dinner and picking up the newspaper from the living room floor, but they don't mind if their husbands do.

Set an atmosphere of romance tonight. Set your table with real plates instead of paper and offer to load the dishwasher when the meal is over. You'll be surprised at how much she will appreciate your thoughtfulness.

Make up your mind to be available for her. Schedule your day so that everything is done by nine o'clock. The number one killer of love is fatigue, but she won't be exhausted if you pitch in and do your share. She will have the energy to be a passionate lover.

Next, be sure the outside of your "car" is prepared. Shower your troubles away at five o'clock. Of course, you'll be shaven and seductive in a thoroughly clean outfit. Perhaps you're thinking, "Since I'm twenty pounds overweight, I don't feel very seductive in skin tight jeans." Stop worrying. She chose you because she loves you. Concentrate on your good qualities and she will too. She won't be able to take her eyes off you. Best of all, she'll know how much you care.

Prepare now for lovemaking tonight. This is one of our class projects. In fact by the second week, the men are prepared for sexual intercourse every night for a week. When I gave the homework in one class, a man muttered audibly, "Doesn't he know there's football on Monday night?"

One Fort Worth husband told how he carefully prepared for love seven nights in a row, "whatever, whenever, and wherever," and it was his wife who couldn't take it. "I don't know what's wrong with you, but I need some sleep. I've got to get up at 5:30. Now be still!"

Communication Not Competition

Communication can restore a bad mood or disagreement. One husband felt that he had been unjustly accused of laziness by his wife. His pride took over and he refused to talk until she begged him. She finally broke the silence by saying, "If you don't pay attention to me, I'm leaving." Watch that you don't allow your foolishness to cause you to lose the woman you adore.

Communicate with your spouse before it's too late. Don't let problems carry over to the next day. There is no place for misunderstandings in a good marriage. Part of her problem may be that she needs to know that you value her opinions. Talk it out and change your attitude. More often than not that's all it takes.

Love never makes demands. Love is unconditional acceptance of her and her feelings. She does not need competition at home. She's had that all day at work. She needs your companionship and moral support instead.

A mature couple does not demand perfection. They do not chase false goals that can only end in disappointment. They are willing to work together to accomplish what is best for both of them.

You can become a Rembrandt in your communication skills. Or you can stay at the finger-painting stage. One wife, by the way, felt her husband was at the kindergartner stage because he always stomped his feet and pouted when he didn't get his own way. The benefits in your becoming a Rembrandt cannot be overemphasized. You can begin now to be a budding artist. Tonight is your night for sensational conversation followed by incredible lovemaking with the woman you adore. Prepare, anticipate, relax and enjoy!

Lesson Number 3: Sex 101

1. Be an atmosphere adjuster in the morning. Pitch in and help with those chores that she simply does not have time for.

2. Once this week send her flowers for no reason. Then take your shower before she comes home.

3. Thrill her at the front door in your clean jeans. Variety is the spice of sex.

4. Be prepared mentally for conversation every night this week.

5. If you feel your situation involves a deeper problem, make the first move to call a marriage counselor yourself. The marriage you save may be your own!

Part Five

REPAIRING BRIDGES

12

Silence Is Not Golden

Honest, open communication is imperative if you want your marriage to succeed. Men and women seem to have different communication styles. A man wants to discuss ideas and dreams; women seem to want to discuss emotion. How often do you tell your wife, "I love you," and anxiously wait for her response? You know she loves you. Hasn't she told you so a thousand times? Yet you continue to say the same thing and need the reassurance of her response again and again.

A man wants an expression of love in words, but a woman expresses her love with actions—by supporting him financially, by providing him with clean clothes and hot meals. He wants words and she gives him monetary peace of mind. Is it any wonder that a communication gap exists between the genders?

A man who believes in communicating with his woman is in great demand. Taking the time to listen to, and understand, the woman you love is an accomplishment you can be proud of. If she knows that you are making a real effort to converse with her, and you are interested in what she has to say, your marriage cannot help but blossom.

Wiser Husbands/Happier Wives

It is not possible for love to flourish if you allow a wall of misunderstanding to grow between you and your wife. Nothing makes a woman feel happier than to know she is understood. She will become a much more confident woman with an understanding mate at her side.

Is there a wall slowly, but steadily, being erected between you and your wife? You can be a wiser husband and have a satisfied wife if you learn to communicate. That wall will crumble to dust at your feet if you are willing to take these simple rules to heart:

1. Listen when she talks. When my wife and I attended family functions, I thought that as soon as she started talking, that was my license to start a conversation with the person seated next to me, or worse yet, standing halfway across the room. My shouting prevented anyone else from communicating with each other. I was no better at home. I would use the remote to flip through all forty-five of the television channels as quickly as possible, or I read the sports page and occasionally muttered, "Mmhm," in response. I honestly believed that I could do whatever I wanted and listen to her with half an ear.

I quickly discovered that she wanted me to really pay attention when she talked. She wanted me to make eye contact with her and to concentrate on what she was saying. She wanted me to respond with intelligent questions and comments. Like most women, she wanted a good listener.

2. Don't offer advice unless she asks for it. No one wants unsolicited advice, your wife included. Much too often husbands give advice that was never asked for such as, "I would never put up with that kind of treatment," or "If my boss said that to me, I'd quit." She's not asking you to tell her what to do. She wants you to listen while she blows off a little steam. Remember, she's not a little girl anymore, and she doesn't need "daddy" to solve her problems. All she wants is for you, the man she loves, to be there when she needs someone to talk to.

3. Don't criticize. As men, we often find it amusing to criticize our spouses in front of others. We think it makes us look like we're the ones in charge. Nobody respects you when you say rude things to your wife, especially not her. It is not cute to cut your wife down in an attempt to build yourself up in front of your buddies. She is the one you will be going home with. She is the woman you live with. Don't build walls that can stop the flow of communication.

4. Understand where she is coming from. Both her frame of reference and her goals are different than yours. Don't expect her to change to conform to your way of thinking.

One wife came home from her monotonous job as a secretary one afternoon and announced to her husband that she wanted to go back to school. His first thought was, "Oh no, there goes half of our income," but he thought before he blurted out this statement and realized she wanted to go back to school to better herself. It was something she had talked about for years. "Good for you," he told her with a sincere smile on his face. "When do you start?" He realized that his plans and hers were not the same and offered the encouragement that she needed.

5. Be sensitive to her feelings. Your wife does not need constant coddling, but she does need your understanding. If she's had a hard day at the office, spent an hour in a traffic jam on the way home from work, and been told by the teller at the bank that her check cannot be cashed this afternoon because the account is overdrawn, she doesn't need extra pressure from you. When she finally makes it through the front door, don't start in with the problems you had with the kids or the checker at the grocery store.

Give her some time to relax and unwind. Offer encouragement and consolation. Give her a hug and tell her things will be better tomorrow. She needs your love and understanding now more than ever.

6. Make her interests your interests. This is not to say that you must do everything together. You are not attached at the hip. But there should be some interests that the two of you share. Don't be afraid to try new things.

If she enjoys the ballet, go with her once in awhile. If she adores the theatre, accompany her to a few plays. She should also have an interest in what you like. If you enjoy going to the flea markets or car shows she should want to go with you once in a while too. You may both be surprised to find that you enjoy activities that you never thought of before. After all, the couple who plays together stays together!

Take a Deep Breath

All marriages have problems at one time or another. There is no such thing as a perfect marriage or a perfect wife. Any couple that tries to tell you they never argue or disagree is probably lying. If you have more than one person in the same home, there will be arguments once in awhile. That's human nature.

How you cope with these problems is the important thing. Do you tend to get furious about every minor disagreement? Do you lose your temper at the slightest provocation? Or do you clam up and give your spouse the silent treatment for hours on end? Screaming won't solve anything, but neither will refusing to talk out the differences.

Yelling will do one of two things. It will either cause your wife to become extremely angry and begin to yell back, or she will tune you out. Either way, nothing gets resolved. Pouting and not speaking only tends to alienate your spouse. She will never tell you anything if you are going to go to extremes.

The next time you and your wife have a disagreement, take a deep breath and remember:

1. Don't scream. Loud arguments don't solve problems. If you both lose your tempers you may end up saying things you will regret later. You'll say something cruel, and then she will retaliate. Women do not enjoy knockdown, drag-out fights, but she will fight back to protect herself. Try to remain calm and rational.

2. Plan the proper time to discuss problems. Think before you speak. If she's just come through the front door with two crying children and a torn bag of groceries clutched under one arm, it is not the time to tell her how frustrated you are because she promised to pick up your good slacks at the cleaners and forgot. Firstly, you should be capable of retrieving your own slacks. Secondly, if you start in on her when she's already feeling harried, she is sure to become angry.

Save your problems until she is in a more compassionate mood. Timing is everything. The best time may be after the children have been put to bed and she has had a chance to sit down and relax for awhile. Explain to her that you have tried to see things her way, and now you would like her to try to understand your side.

3. Stick to the problem at hand. It may be tempting to bring up past problems, but don't! "Last week you," or "Remember when you" does not solve the problem at hand. It will only make her defensive and she will not want to discuss the current situation. Concentrate on the here and now.

4. Forgive and Forget. This may be the most difficult thing to do, but it will be well worth it. Forgiving means wiping the slate clean. Past mistakes are to be forgotten and not brought up over and over again. The man who does not learn to forgive will never have a happy marriage.

Remember that your attitude toward solving problems helps determine your wife's outlook as well. If you are angry, she will become angry. If you clam up and refuse to speak, you will alienate her. If you approach each problem as it arises with the attitude that the two of you can work through anything, she will feel the same. Confidence builds the communication skills you both need in order to have a home that is a shelter from the rest of the world, and not a battlefield.

Part Six

COUNT YOUR BLESSINGS

13

Count Them One By One

Not every married couple has or wants children, and this is certainly their choice. No one should ever try to make him or her feel guilty or insist that they don't know what they are missing. They do know what they are missing! Raising children is a full-time job and this may well be the reason they have decided not to have any. Whatever their reasons, they are their own and they are not obligated to explain their reasons to anyone: not his parents or her parents, or anyone else. If you do have children, you should consider them blessings. The Bible tells us that "Children are an heritage of the Lord: and the fruit of the womb is his reward," (Psalm 127:3). Children should never be viewed as burdens you must bear until they reach the age of eighteen (or twenty-one or twenty-five!) and leave home. The attitude you have about raising your children will determine what kind of adults they become.

Judge Not

Accepting your child for what she (or he) is will do wonders for her self-esteem. Don't try to change her to fit some preconceived notion you have of what she should be. If you've always dreamed of having a dentist in the family, but she wants to become a journalist, encourage her. Maybe your wife wanted to be the head cheerleader in high school or you wanted to be a star football player, but these may not be things your children are interested in. You had your chance to pursue your dreams; maybe you didn't reach all of them, but give your kids the same opportunity.

The worst mistake you can make as a parent is comparing one child to another. She will become resentful of the sibling she is being compared to, and she will also end up disliking you. Remember that each child is an individual. Each one will have her own faults as well as talents. If she is not accepted for herself, she will grow up feeling insecure and inadequate.

Mr. Thompson wanted his daughter to become a ballerina even though she had her heart set on being a surgeon. He had once dated a dancer in college and remembered how lovely she had looked dancing in Swan Lake. He constantly dragged his daughter to dance classes that she had no desire to attend. The little girl decided, "I'll never be able to do what Dad wants. I can hardly wait until I leave home. Someday I'll find someone who will accept me exactly as I am."

Praise Her

Praise is the strongest builder of self-esteem that you can offer your child. Don't dwell on her mistakes—we all make them. Don't expect more out of her than she can give. If she makes a C in biology and you know she has given her all, compliment her for a job well done. Don't ask why she didn't make an A. If she presents you with a hand-made gift, don't criticize it. Tell her how beautiful it is and put it in a place where everyone can see it.

Too many parents tend to dwell on children's mistakes instead of their good points. If this is part of your parenting style, stop it at once! Your approval and praise will give her the confidence she needs to become a wonderful, caring adult.

Love Her

Unconditional love is the greatest gift you can give your child. All the presents in the world will not make her truly happy if she doesn't know that you love her no matter what happens. She needs to hear you say, "I love you" every day and she needs you to show her.

Give her daily hugs, even when—no especially when—she is a teenager. She may pull away and make faces (teenagers don't always like their parents, and that's okay), but your constant reassurance that you love her will give her the support she needs. If she knows that your love is constant, she will feel comfortable in approaching you with questions about sex or drugs or anything else that may concern her.

Play Together

You may not be able to afford extravagant vacations to Disneyland, but you can still spend time with your children. Take them to the park, or to the zoo. Assist them with school projects; take them to the library on a weekly basis. Get involved in their lives. Find out what they like to do and do it with them. You are their father and they need you in their lives as much as they need their mother. Why not be the one who tucks them into bed every night and reads them a story? You may be surprised how much you enjoy it.

If you have a hobby, get your children involved. Teach your daughter how to build a model ship, or to tell the difference between a wren and a sparrow. Make her a part of your daily life. If she wants to play baseball, play with her. If she is ready to learn how to drive, you teach her. Remember to be patient and loving with her; she will make mistakes, but so do you!

Set Limits

Believe it or not, your children want you to set limits for them. Yes, they will test you from time to time, but they need to know that you care about what they do. You and your wife must present a united front. If she sets a rule, you must not break it "just this once" because you don't want to be seen as the "bad guy."

Establish rules and tell your children why. Never use "because I said so." That is not a reason, and your daughter will not understand. If you don't want her to spend the night at a friend's house because you know her parents are not going to be home, tell the truth. Let your daughter know that you do not believe she is old enough to be alone at night unsupervised. She may get angry, but at least she'll know why she cannot go.

Remember that rules are not written in stone. There are times when you and your wife can agree to change something. If the rule is that your daughter must be home every night at eleven, but a movie she wants to see with her friends doesn't end until midnight, you can bend the rules to fit the occasion. This is not the same as being inconsistent. Inconsistent means that things are never the same. She gets punished for something one time and ignored for it the next.

Let your children know how much you care about them, but at the same time let them know there are limits. Some behavior is acceptable and some is not. Let your daughter know that she has your trust.

If you expect her to do something wrong, she probably will. Children live up, or down to our expectations. Expect the best and that is probably what you will get. Until she does something wrong, don't worry about it. Don't be judgmental or overly harsh in your punishments. Be interested in her life, but don't monitor her every move or question every decision. Above all, let her know that you love her and will always be there for her.

Testing The Waters

I recently had lunch with a close friend who was experiencing some emotional difficulties. He remembered how, as a little boy, he watched his parents' reactions if he broke the rules. If they failed to discipline him, he thought they were afraid of him and honestly believed he could do whatever he wanted. One day when he was sixteen, he threw a temper tantrum because his mother told him he was not allowed to drive her car. She finally threw up her hands in disgust and said, "Fine, take the car. Take whatever you want. I don't really care what you do." That statement was a turning point in his life. He came to the conclusion that his mother did not love him because she failed to regulate his behavior. She did not care enough to make him behave. Because no one cared enough to offer him guidance when he wanted to test the waters, this man now finds self-control extremely difficult. He thinks he should have whatever his heart desires, whenever he wants it.

In another case, a teenager deliberately broke curfew to go to a movie with his friends. When he finally got home, his father was tired and decided to overlook the infraction this one time and told his son to go to bed. The next morning the son received a call from a friend asking him to go to the mall. The father overheard the boy telling his friend he couldn't go "because I stayed out too late last night and I'm grounded today." He felt guilty because he had disobeyed his parents who always trusted him to do the right thing. It was easier for this boy to punish himself than to carry around the burden of remorse he was feeling for breaking the rules.

Studies indicate that children who grow up without limits cannot control themselves in a consistent manner as adults. They feel unloved and frustrated and often behave negatively just to receive attention.

As your child grows, she will be compelled to test the waters, to see how much you will let her get away with. It is up to you to offer disci-

pline and to set reasonable boundaries for your child. Discipline is train-
ing. Adults often equate discipline with spanking or some other sort of
punishment, but this is not true. Discipline is positive. Discipline consists
of two things: setting guidelines and correcting when a child sidesteps
the rules. A parent who is afraid to discipline because he does not want
his child to be angry with him is only asking for heartache.

Let your child know what is expected of him. He may balk occasionally, but he will feel secure in knowing what he can and cannot get
away with. When a touchy situation comes up with friends, it is often
easier for a child to say, "My parents won't let me go there," than to have
to lie and act cool. Other kids have parents who set limits too, so they
will understand even if they don't like it. A parent's love protects a child
from harm by keeping him safe within the boundaries set by his family.

Don't feel bad if your family does not agree on every issue. To
expect total harmony is unrealistic and will only add stress to your life.
Your children will have different ideas than you do about what is right
and what is wrong. A son became very angry with his father who refused
to let him attend a late night party. "I know you don't agree with me and
think I should let you go," the father explained. "But, I don't know these
people and the party starts past your curfew. I would worry too much if
I let you go." He did not expect his son to agree with him, but he took
the time to explain his convictions.

Children may not like to admit you're right, but you have to do what
you think is best for them. Parenting is not a popularity contest. Your
child may often be angry with you and may tell you she doesn't like you.
Keep in mind that you probably didn't like your parents all of the time
either. As long as you know you are doing what is best for your child,
don't give in.

If you must punish a child for disobeying, remember to explain to
her that you still love her, but do not approve of her behavior. Never use
extreme or harsh punishment to discipline your child. Set the punishment
to meet the crime. Should she really lose phone privileges for a month
because she stayed out twenty minutes past curfew?

By testing the waters, your child will learn to take responsibility for
her actions. This is the goal you are striving for—a responsible adult.

Accept Her Friends

Maybe they have long hair or even no hair. The boys might wear earrings
and makeup on occasion. They might all wear baggy clothes and carry

backpacks wherever they go. Don't pass judgement based on their appearance.

Take the time to get to know them. You may be pleasantly surprised to find out how intelligent and sensitive these kids are. It doesn't matter that they listen to music by bands you never heard of who sing lyrics you cannot understand. Your daughter chose these friends and you trust her judgement, right? Her friends are an important part of her life, so make them a part of your life too, but don't go overboard. Don't decide that it would be fun to hang out with the kids at the mall or invite yourself to accompany them to the movies. They want to know that you approve of them, but they do not want you to be their best buddy.

Talk To Her

I know you have a busy life and it is often hard to take the time to really talk with your child, but it is imperative that you communicate with her. You may become frustrated at first because she may be uncommunicative, but keep trying. If you have never taken the time to show an interest in what she has to say, she may be a little suspicious of your motives.

Don't give up. Keep trying. Ask her about her day. When she answers you, listen to her responses. Ask questions. Let her know that you are genuinely interested in what she is saying. Encourage her to ask you questions too. Make talking with your child an important part of your day.

Encourage Her

A busy father of three encouraged his youngest daughter to sing even though she couldn't carry a tune at all. The more she sang, the more praise he gave. The little girl developed confidence in herself, took voice lessons and is now a soloist in her high school choir.

Your child has an image of herself, just as you have one of yourself. She determines her self-worth from your words and actions and begins to become like the image she has of herself whether it is good or bad. If you continually tell her, "You are so stupid," she'll grow up believing she is stupid. If you constantly ask, "What is the matter with you?" she will begin to think there really is something wrong with her.

If you offer constant encouragement and support, she will believe that she can accomplish anything. Everyone loves encouragement. If you have been in the habit of criticizing, this may be difficult at first, but keep trying. In the long run, your effort will be well worth the results.

It is virtually impossible to overpraise or love your child too much. Praise does not spoil a child and love only encourages her to blossom. Begin today to shower that tender flower of yours with love and compliments. If she is not exposed to sunshine on a daily basis, she may wither up inside.

Parents should view their children as gifts from God. Children should feel the love their parents have for them and know that there is very little they can do that would cause parents to lose faith in them. We want our children to believe that they can do anything that they set their minds to.

Your child should feel proud of who she is and where she comes from. Maybe you didn't have a lot of confidence when you were a child, but you can make sure your children do. Build your child up at every opportunity. Never discourage her from trying. Let her know how much you believe in her abilities.

Happy Days

When she was twelve, Kelly was sent to a church camp in east Texas. Every day her parents checked their mailbox hoping for a letter from her. Finally, after almost two weeks, a letter arrived that read:

> Dear Mom and Dad,
> My counselor said I had to write to you before
> I could have breakfast. So here is my letter.
>
> Love, Kelly

This may not be your idea of communication, but it was to the counselor. The goal of communication is not to have total agreement between the parties, but understanding. Kelly's parents knew that she was okay and enjoying herself, otherwise she would have spelled out her unhappiness in no uncertain terms. Understanding is the ability to see things from the other person's viewpoint. It is the ability to understand why the other person does and says the things she does.

In order to understand your child you must be willing to bridge the communication gap. For parents, this involves more listening than talking. Your child knows that if you love her, you will listen to her. The following suggestions may help you to become a better listener:

1. Be available. Children need us to listen when they are ready to talk. If you are too busy, she may be gone when you are ready to listen. Set priorities. Is it more important to read the sports page right now or listen to what your daughter has to say?

2. Be interesting to talk to. Each day at dinner, our family shares a pleasant experience. Everyone is encouraged to remember one good thing that happened during the day and share it with the rest of us.

My wife and I also share our life stories with the children. It helps open the lines of communication if we are honest, so we tell our mistakes and failures along with the fun times. One evening I told our oldest daughter about my mom grounding me for two weeks because I had lied to her. She loved to hear how I had gotten in trouble for disobeying one of the rules and asked me to tell that story over and over. She is now old enough to tell funny stories about her childhood to her younger sister.

3. Be flexible and listen to the child's side of the story. At a friend's house recently, I overheard the father effectively cut off communication between himself and his daughter by saying, "As long as you live under my roof, you'll think what I tell you to think." Instead of insisting that your child have the same opinions that you do, keep the communication flowing by letting her know that you value her opinions. If you have a close, honest relationship with your child, she will not want to hurt you or upset you. If you tend to blow up over everything, she will soon lose respect for you. She wants you to be secure in your position, but she needs you to be flexible enough to hear hers. If you remain closed-minded, she will think she is not allowed to express her opinion, especially about sex and drugs, two of the areas she may have the most questions about.

If she does share with you, don't run to a friend with her confidences. If she finds out that you are sharing her intimate secrets with your friends she will no longer confide in you. If you care about your relationship with your child, respect her enough to keep secrets between the two of you no matter how cute or interesting they may be.

Recall from a previous section that I stressed how important communication between you and your wife is. It is just as important in your relationship with your child. If you don't communicate with her, you have no way of knowing what is happening in her life.

Child Rearing Rules

1. Accept her for what she is. Don't try to mold her into what you think she should be.

2. Let her know how much you love her. Show her with words and actions.

3. Enjoy her. Spend time with her every day.

4. Play with her, read to her, and be there.

5. Set limits and let her know why. There are rules and there are reasons.

6. Trust her. She deserves your trust until she does something to prove otherwise.

7. Encourage her. Let her know how proud you are of her accomplishments. Let her know that you believe she can do anything that she sets her mind to.

8. Keep the lines of communication open. Be there when she needs to talk and listen to what she has to say.

9. Most importantly, praise her. Praise her! Praise her!

Don't be too hard on yourself. You will make mistakes as a parent— we all do. When you mess up, don't be afraid to admit it. Saying "I'm sorry," and being sincere about it can make a difference. If you do the best that you can and your child still has problems, it is not always your fault. Children are individuals and make their own choices as they grow. If something comes up that you cannot handle don't be afraid to seek professional help. You or your child, or possibly both, could benefit from the advice of a trained professional. Don't wait until it is too late to make a difference in your child's life.

Part Seven

LOCATING YOUR SOURCE OF POWER

14

Organized Religion

At this point, I would like to be able to say, "Take your troubles to God and everything will be fine," but I believe that would be a cop-out. In this day and age organized religion is not a pat answer for everyone. There are thousands of people who have never attended a church service, or who, for one reason or another, have turned away from religion as a source of inspiration and power. What happens to them if I simply say, "God will provide"? More than likely they will toss this book aside in disgust and mutter under their breath about it being the same old tripe that has been handed out for years. I don't want that. Keep reading! I will get to you in a minute.

If, however you are active in church, you know that prayers and fellowship with others who share your beliefs can be a great source of inspiration. You can literally, "Take your troubles to God," and find comfort in knowing he will provide the guidance and support you need when you are not sure whether you can go on or not.

It is difficult to change your life, and sometimes you will believe that you cannot go on. It is so much easier to say, "I can't," than to keep striving toward a goal that seems almost impossible. At times of great stress and doubt, remember that God offers peace to a troubled soul: "Peace I leave with you, my peace I give unto you: not as the world giveth, give I unto you. Let not your heart be troubled, neither let it be afraid." (*John 14:27*) Take comfort in knowing that God wants to lift your burdens and fears and He is there for you when you need him. Turn to Him in times of trouble and doubt and He will supply the reassurance you need to change your life and attitudes.

Spend time in fellowship with other members of your congregation. Their faith and belief that God will guide them through anything can be a source of inspiration for you. Does your church offer marriage counseling? Talk to your minister or priest—ask for his support and prayers. He will be pleased to know that you are working to improve your relationship with your spouse and he can offer spiritual guidance.

Getting Back To Nature

As I mentioned earlier, organized religion is not the answer for everyone, but each of us needs something or someone to turn to in times of trouble and stress. What makes you feel better about yourself? What activities renew your spirit and set your feet back on track?

Carol, a close friend of ours, did not grow up attending church on a regular basis. She occasionally attended services with friends, but her family never placed any emphasis on a need for organized religion.

Carol married a man who came from a very religious background. He had attended church every Sunday as a child, and it was important to both him and his family that Carol become a church member. She agreed.

She became very active in the church and was very happy. She did volunteer work, and taught a children's bible class every Sunday morning before services. Everyone in the congregation knew Carol and they were pleased that she had become a part of their church family.

After several years of marriage, and two small children, Carol's marriage began to crumble. After much agonizing and soul-searching, she and her husband agreed to divorce. Carol and her daughters moved to another town and began to attend another church.

Carol expressed an interest in teaching bible class, and the elders of the church arranged to meet with her and discuss her plans. The meeting took place in a private room of the church and Carol was told how happy she had made the elders by offering her services. She was handed a videotape that explained how the teaching program in the church worked and advised to watch it carefully. The group continued to talk, and somehow the subject of Carol's recent divorce came up. One of the elders stood, and unceremoniously jerked the videotape from Carol's hands. "We do not allow divorced women to teach in our church!"

Carol was flabbergasted. She did not try to defend herself. She left the room, found her children and walked out of the church. Except for the occasional wedding or funeral, she has refused to set foot in a church building. Her faith in the church and its members as a means of support and love was lost.

Carol felt lost and alone, and didn't know where to turn. One Sunday afternoon, while her daughters were visiting their father, she decided to take a drive in the country. She came upon a secluded, wooded area and decided to get out and take a walk. She spent two hours walking among the trees and listening to the birds call back and forth to one another. "At that time," Carol said, "I felt more at peace with myself than I had in months. Any time I feel like the pressures of every day living are getting out of hand, I drive out to that little spot and spend a couple of hours. I come home feeling refreshed and ready to meet any challenge that comes my way."

Carol has found a new source of power. Communing with nature relieves her stress and helps her to carry on.

Another friend told me that whenever he is feeling stressed he goes fishing. Being alone on the quiet lake gives him the time to work through his problems. He usually concludes that things are not as bad as he had originally thought. He goes home feeling refreshed and ready to face the coming week.

Do you have something to turn to in times of stress and doubt? Something that will renew your confidence in yourself and help you to keep moving forward? Maybe nature is not the answer for you. Can you turn to your friends or family? Is there someone you can talk with and explain your problems to? Will they listen without passing judgement and offer advice when you want it? A supportive network of friends, who understand your desire to change, may be the power source you are searching for.

Above all, do not give up. Keep searching for that special source that will revitalize you and give you the will to keep trying. You can do it!

Part Eight

PHYSICAL FITNESS AND DIET

15

Exercise Your Way To Happiness

Women are more understanding when it comes to a few extra inches here and there, but that doesn't mean she wants you to turn into a total slob. When was the last time you were involved in some type of physical activity? No, using your thumb to push the buttons on the remote control does not count. Neither does walking from the parking lot to the office building.

Since 1990, death rates from coronary heart disease (CHD) continue to decrease for men and women in the United States, but heart disease is still the leading cause of mortality in the United States. In California, 42 percent of all deaths were attributable to cardiovascular disease (CVD) for the 3-year period of 1989-1991. Among CVD deaths, 70 percent were due either to CHD or stroke (California Governor's Council on Physical Fitness and Sports). Don't become a statistic—start exercising before it is too late!

You enjoy watching sports on television, but when was the last time you were a participant and not an observer? Now is the time to devise an exercise routine of your own.

Do you like to play golf? Why not walk the course instead of riding in a cart? Does your company have a softball team? Why not join? It will not only be pleasurable, but it will provide you with a lot of physical activity.

Okay, so you don't like organized sports. Can you walk? Why not take a brisk walk every morning after you get the kids off to school? Better yet, why not wait until the evening and walk with your family? Not only will you become more physically fit, you can spend more time with your children and your spouse. Walking is wonderful exercise and it is very inexpensive.

You can join a health club or swim at the local YMCA. If the idea of exercising in a room full of sweaty people in tight clothes turns you off, invest in a treadmill and use it. Walk a couple of miles on it every day. It won't be long before you begin to notice a difference in both your appearance and the way you feel. You can also buy exercise videos, or check them out at the library, and use them in the privacy of your own living room.

The old cliché, "If you look good, you feel good," still holds true. Better physical health will also give you more energy to participate in the daily routine of chasing after little kids. Let's face it, taking care of little Jeffy and his sister Sue is a tough job. You'll feel better knowing that you can keep up with them.

I'm not telling you to become a fitness junky, but exercise is an essential part of a healthy life. If you want to spend many more years with your family, start taking care of your body today!

Healthy Eating

Yes, I know how much you like to devour a bag of corn chips as you sit on the couch and watch Dallas beat Seattle one more time. Or how much fun it is to eat foot-long franks at the baseball game on a hot July afternoon. You enjoy ice cream and cold beer in the summer time and bowls of steaming hot chili when the temperatures began to drop, but how healthy are you? A good diet is the starting point of a healthier, happier you. Experts agree the key to healthy eating is the time-tested advice of balance, variety and moderation. In short, that means eating a wide variety of foods without getting too many calories or too much of any one nutrient. These 10 tips can help you follow that advice while still enjoying the foods you eat (Cosponsored by: The American Dietetic Association, April, 1994).

1. Eat a variety of nutrient-rich foods. You need more than 40 different nutrients for good health, and no single food supplies them all. Your daily food selection should include bread and other whole-grain products; fruits; vegetables; dairy products; and meat, poultry, fish and other protein foods. How much you should eat depends on your calorie needs. Use the Food Guide Pyramid and the Nutrition Facts panel on food labels as handy references.

2. Enjoy plenty of whole grains, fruits and vegetables. Surveys show most Americans don't eat enough of these foods. Do you eat 6-11 servings from the bread, rice, cereal and pasta group, 3 of which should be whole grains? Do you eat 2-4 servings of fruit and 3-5 servings of vegetables? If you don't enjoy some of these at first, give them another chance. Look through cookbooks for tasty ways to prepare unfamiliar foods.

3. Maintain a healthy weight. The weight that's right for you depends on many factors including your sex, height, age and heredity. Excess body fat increases your chances for high blood pressure, heart disease, stroke, diabetes, some types of cancer and other illnesses. But being too thin can increase your risk for osteoporosis and other health problems. If you're constantly losing and regaining weight, a registered dietitian can help you develop sensible eating habits for successful weight management. Regular exercise is also important to maintaining a healthy weight.

4. Eat moderate portions. If you keep portion sizes reasonable, it's easier to eat the foods you want and stay healthy. Did you know the recommended serving of cooked meat is 3 ounces, similar in size to a deck of playing cards? A medium piece of fruit is 1 serving and a cup of pasta equals 2 servings. A pint of ice cream contains 4 servings.

5. Eat regular meals. Skipping meals can lead to out-of-control hunger, often resulting in overeating. When you're very hungry, it's also tempting to forget about good nutrition. Snacking between meals can help curb hunger, but don't eat so much that your snack becomes an entire meal.

6. Reduce, don't eliminate, certain foods. Most people eat for pleasure as well as nutrition. If your favorite foods are high in fat, salt or sugar, the key is moderating how much of these foods you eat and how often you eat them. Identify major sources of these ingredients in your diet and make changes, if necessary. Adults who eat high-fat meats or whole-milk dairy products at every meal are probably eating too much fat. Use the Nutrition Facts panel on the food label to help balance your choices. Choosing skim or low-fat dairy products and lean cuts of meat, such as flank steak and beef round, can reduce fat intake significantly. If you love fried chicken, however, you don't have to give it up. Just eat it less often. When dining out, share it with a friend, or ask for a take-home bag or a smaller portion.

7. Balance your food choices over time. Not every food has to be "perfect." When eating a food high in fat, salt or sugar, select other foods that are low in these ingredients. If you miss out on any food group one day, make up for it the next. Your food choices over several days should fit together into a healthy pattern.

8. Know your diet pitfalls. To improve your eating habits, you first have to know what's wrong with them. Write down everything you eat for three days. Then check your list according to the rest of these tips. Do you add a lot of butter, creamy sauces or salad dressings? Rather than eliminating these foods, just cut back your portions. Are you getting enough fruits and vegetables? If not, you may be missing out on vital nutrients.

9. Make changes gradually. Just as there are no "superfoods" or easy answers to a healthy diet, don't expect to totally revamp your eating habits overnight. Changing too much, too fast can get in the way of success. Begin to remedy excesses or deficiencies with modest changes that can add up to positive, lifelong eating habits. For instance, if you don't like the taste of skim milk, try low-fat. Eventually you may find you like skim, too.

10. Remember, foods are not good or bad. Select foods based on your total eating patterns, not whether any individual food is "good" or "bad." Don't feel guilty if you love foods such as apple pie, potato chips, candy bars or ice cream. Eat them in moderation, and choose other foods to provide the balance and variety that are vital to good health.

Figuring Out Fat

With so much information available about the effects of dietary fat on health, understanding the role fat plays in a well-balanced diet can be pretty confusing. To cut through the confusion, it's important to remember that fat is an essential nutrient that everyone needs to stay healthy. Fat is a valuable energy source and carries fat-soluble vitamins needed for proper growth and development. It also contributes important taste and textural qualities that are part of enjoying food.

Too much fat, however, can increase the risk of heart disease, obesity and other health problems. When moderating fat intake, it's important to consider these points: Health authorities recommend Americans consume 30 percent or less of their total daily calories from fat, with 10 percent or less of those calories from saturated fat. Remember, the 30 percent refers to your total fat intake over time, not single foods or meals. Use the following chart to guide your fat intake:

Table 15.1

If you eat this number of calories per day:	Total fat per day (grams)	Total saturated fat per day grams)
1,600	53 or less	18 or less
2,000	65 or less	20 or less
2,200	73 or less	24 or less
2,500	80 or less	25 or less

Use the Nutrition Facts panel on the food label to help determine how much fat is in foods. Remember, it's the total fat intake over time that's important. A food high in fat can be part of a healthy diet as long as it's balanced with other lower-fat food choices. (Reprinted from the International Food Information Council Foundation and the American Dietetic Association, 1994).

Sounds like a lot to remember, but, one more time, you can do it. By becoming physically fit and eating right, you will become happier with yourself. If you are more confident, you cannot help but feel better about the relationship with your wife. By now, you truly are on your way to becoming a Total Man!

Conclusion

It would be virtually impossible to explain the Total Man concept in a fifteen-minute conversation. It is often difficult to explain it in a four-week course. Total Man is a way of life, a change in attitude, and a new outlook toward yourself, your wife and your children.

Total Man starts with the premise that every man can change and become a better, more loving husband and parent if he really wants to. No man needs to go through life in a loveless marriage.

A Total Man has no qualms about doing housework or being an active participant in the lives of his children. He is an attentive lover and a good friend.

A Total Man has respect for both himself and his partner. He knows how hard she works and he appreciates her efforts. He is not afraid to let her know that he needs her in his life. He knows that he would feel incomplete without her.

He encourages his wife to reach for the stars and he is there to give her a boost if she falls. By encouraging her to become the best she can be, he knows that she will be a happier, more productive woman.

No one expects you to become a Total Man overnight. You may slip up and fall back into your old patterns. That's okay. Start fresh in the morning with the determination to change both your attitude and your outlook. You will be a happier and more satisfied man if you decide to really change your life. You and your wife can look forward to many years of happiness together. This is not to say you won't run into snags every once in a while—you will. Don't give up! It takes time to change a lifetime of bad habits, but you can do it if you really want to.

Keep these simple rules in mind:

1. Don't dwell on the past. By this point you have become a new man. There is no reason to regret the things you did wrong or worry about what you could have done differently. The past is past—move on.

2. Don't be discouraged. You are bound to slip up once in awhile. Old habits are hard to break. Apologize for your mistakes and move on. Don't give up!

3. Remember how much potential you have. Your wife chose you, not someone else. She knew that you were, and still are, something special. You can accomplish anything if you set your mind to it. Keep trying.

I wouldn't dream of telling you that following my guidelines will guarantee perfect success, but I do believe that if the changes I have made in my life worked for me, they can work for you, too. I have also stressed the importance of seeking professional help, be it from a marriage counselor or a psychiatrist, whenever necessary. Don't ever be ashamed to admit that you cannot handle a situation on your own. After all, each of us is aiming for the same thing—a happier, more successful marriage—and I hope that you will find it.

Yes, even you can become the Total Man you have always dreamed of being. Good Luck and God Bless!

Bibliography

California Governor's Council on Physical Fitness. Online. Alta Vista. Available 07/07/97. hc2000.html#obj1.

Chafetz, Janet Saltzman. "I Need a Traditional Wife: Employment-Family Conflicts." Workplace/Women's Place: An Anthology. Ed. Dana Dunn. Los Angeles: Roxbury Publishing Company. 1997. 116-123.

International Food Information Council Foundation. 1100 Connecticut Avenue, N.W. Suite 430. Washington, DC 20036. (Cosponsored by the American Dietetic Association, 1994).

Morgan, Marabel. The Total Woman. New York: Simon & Schuster. 1973.

Missildine, W. Hugh. Your Inner Child of the Past. New York: Simon & Schuster. 1991.

Naves Topical Bible. Ed. Orville J. Nave, A.M., D.D., LL.D. Virginia: MacDonald Publishing Company.

Reskin, Barbara and Padavic, Irene. Women and Men at Work. Thousand Oaks, CA.: Pine Forge Press. 1994.

Shelton, Beth Anne. Women, Men, and Time: Gender Differences in Paid Work, Housework, and Leisure. New York: Greenwood Press. 1992.
Tournier, Paul. To Understand Each Other. Virginia: John Knox Press. 1988.

Notes

[1] To the best of my knowledge there is not a company called Bender Glass. James M. Becker and Herman Lee are fictitious characters based on Charles M. Schwab and Ivy Lee. Mr. Schwab was the president of Bethlehem Steel and Ivy Lee was a management consultant.

[2] This letter is based on an actual letter sent to well-known advice columnist, Ann Landers.

[3] This letter is also based on an actual letter to Ann Landers.